COLUM CILLE AND THE COLUMBAN TRADITION

Colum Cille

and the Columban Tradition

Brian Lacey

For CLLR Julian Wates
Mayor of Luton
With best wishes

Brian Lacey
25/5/06

FOUR COURTS PRESS

This book was typeset
in 10 on 12 point Ehrhardt for
FOUR COURTS PRESS
55 Prussia Street, Dublin 7, Ireland
e-mail: fcp@ indigo.ie
and in North America for
FOUR COURTS PRESS
c/o ISBS, 5804 N.E. Hassalo Street, Portland, OR 97213.

A catalogue record for this title
is available from the British Library.

ISBN 1-85182-321-2

Printed in Ireland by ColourBooks Ltd, Dublin.

Contents

Introduction

I protest that, for the miraculous deeds and gifts ascribed in this
little book to certain servants of God, I claim no other belief than
that which is ordinarily given to history resting on mere human
authority; and that, in giving the appellation of Saint or Blessed to
any person not canonized or beatified by the Church, I only intend
to do it according to the usage and opinion of men.

Father William Doherty, 1899

Colum Cille or Columba has been venerated as a 'saint' for nearly a millenium
and a half. He was never canonised, and much of his special status is
derived from tradition and local folklore. Nevertheless, without any doubt
he was a very influential and, indeed, a 'saintly' man and, from shortly
after his death, his reputation for holiness, as well as other virtues and
abilities, was cultivated and celebrated in literary form. To his successor,
Adomnán – the ninth abbot of Iona, at the end of the seventh century –
Colum Cille was unambiguously Saint Columba. He has retained that
distinction ever since.

Whether that honorific title is accepted or not, and even whether or not
it is accepted that there can be such a thing as a 'saint', Colum Cille stands
out as one of the most important figures of the sixth century, and of the
early history of these islands. The impact which he and his followers made,
not only in the religious sphere but in many other aspects of contemporary
culture, such as what we would call the visual arts, literature, history, as
well as what we would now know as international relations, would be
difficult to overestimate. It is little wonder that he has been so much
honoured over such a long time.

Since Colum Cille died in 597, people have been writing in praise of
him, both in secular and religious terms, and in poetry as well as prose.
Despite this vast accumulation of texts, it would still not be possible to
write a modern biography of him. Many of the stories about his life are
legendary in content and written many hundreds of years, and in one
outstanding case as much as a thousand years, later. A study of Colum
Cille is, in that sense, a study of his legacy, a study of what he left to his
successors and what each successive generation in turn has made of his
story over the fourteen hundred years since his death. Much of what was
subsequently written, far from clarifying the events of his life for us actually distorts them. However, these later works testify to the enormous
affection with which the memory of him has been held down the centu-

ries. Also, they often, incidentally, tell us a great deal about the times in which they were written and about the state of the cult of the saint at those times.

The principal problem in attempting to wrest sixth-century fact from the well-meaning, but later, fiction is that of finding authentic sources. We have a vast amount of texts purporting to deal with Colum Cille and his followers. It is not too much of an exaggeration to say that since the saint's day there has been, almost in the manner of Joyce and Yeats, a Colum Cille 'industry'. However, the fundamental question remains: how much, if anything, do these works tell us about events in the sixth century, or relevant later periods of time?

Colum Cille is mentioned briefly in the documents known as the annals. These normally provide us with the skeletal outline of early Irish history, but the extent to which we can rely on them as contemporary evidence for the sixth century is still the subject of analysis and debate. We also have some, fairly, reliable genealogical material which can be used to identify the family connections of Colum Cille and those associated with him. The Venerable Bede (673-735) mentions Columba and his followers frequently in his *Historia Ecclesiastica* ('History of the English Church and People') written in 731. There are three so-called 'Lives' of Colum Cille, unfortunately none of which provide us with a straightforward narrative account of his life. Adomnán's Life was written in Latin towards the end of the seventh century. In the second half of the twelfth century an anonymous, Derry-based author wrote another Life of the saint in Irish. Finally in 1532, the soon-to-be chieftain of the O'Donnells, Manus, collected a huge amount of information about the saint and had a major Life composed, also in the Irish language. In the intervals between these three seminal works, other material was written, and versions and abridgements of the older texts were circulated and copied, not alone in Ireland, but in Britain and on the continent. Much of this literature was unashamedly propagandistic, written as much on behalf of the institution or place and time of its origin as on behalf of its sixth-century subject. Even Adomnán the greatest of Colum Cille's 'biographers', who was closest to him in time and seemingly in spirituality, was not totally innocent of such a motive. Adomnán too was clearly a very 'saintly' man and was himself later venerated as a saint. In reading the Life he wrote about his predecessor, it is sometimes difficult to separate the ideas of the author from those of his subject. While some may think the parallel strained, there is more than a hint of a similarity to the sort of relationship that exists between the ideas of Socrates and the writings of Plato.

The great English historian of the early Irish church, Kathleen Hughes, said of Adomnán's method of composition that it was marked by 'the frequent borrowings of words and phrases, sometimes sentences,' from older works on the Lives of such saints as Anthony, Martin and Jerome. At least in that respect this work is following in the Columban tradition as it certainly owes a great deal to the authors, ancient as well as contemporary, who have written about the saint and his followers. No one has done more in recent times to make our task of understanding the Columban inheritance more easy than Máire Herbert. Both in her work on the individual texts and in her general approach, she has taught us, literally, how to 'read' the original Columban material in order to get at its true historical meaning. We are indebted also to all those who have provided modern, annotated translations of the original works such as A.O. and M.O. Anderson and Richard Sharpe. All of these authors as well as countless others have acknowledged their indebtedness to William Reeves who was working in a supremely scholarly way on these texts one hundred and fifty years ago. I gave up trying to remember how many times I thought I had discovered a new idea about this subject only to find that Reeves had published it already in the 1850s.

This work does not claim to be a substitute for any of the accounts mentioned above. Instead it attempts to make a digest of what is known about Colum Cille and the 'institution' which he founded as it evolved through subsequent history, and to describe something about the way the memory and legacy of Colum Cille was passed on in literature, in art, in folklore, and even in the landscape itself. Of necessity, it has had to be sceptical about some of the best known stories concerning the saint, but these stories are still included and related to what the ancient *Liber Hymnorum* calls the *causa*, the reason or cause why they were written or composed. If there is a critical approach here to the saint's life it is nevertheless made with affection and praise.

The Columban legacy is, itself, one of praise-poetry and story-telling. Manus O'Donnell attributed the defence of that legacy to none other than Colum Cille himself. At the Convention of Drum Ceat the saint was said to have been asked to give his 'judgement' on whether the kings should continue to support the place of poets and poetry in Ireland. In his reply he claimed the highest possible precedent: 'For know you that God himself bought three-fifties of Psalms of praise from King David ... And on that account it is right for you to buy the poems of the poets and to keep the poets in Ireland. And as all the world is but a fable, it were well for you to buy the more enduring fable rather than the one that is less enduring.' And he made this quatrain:

> If poet's verses be but fables,
> So be food and garments fables,
> So is all the world a fable,
> So is man of dust a fable.

I

Colum Cille's Birth and Early Life

> On the seventh day of December Colum Cille was born and on the
> ninth day of June he died. And fitting to his life was the season he
> came into it, for wintry was his life in respect of cold and darkness,
> pain and penance ... And fitting to the life he entered from this
> world was the season when he died, for it is the season that is
> purest and warmest and brightest and most shining of all the year.
>
> Manus O'Donnell, Betha Colaim Chille

Just to the north east of the Derryveagh and Glendowan mountain ranges,
which occupy the centre of County Donegal, is the townland of Lacknacoo.
The area lies on the lower foot-hills of the mountains and overlooks a
cluster of three beautiful lakes, Lough Nacally, Lough Akibbon and, the
largest of the three, Gartan Lough. Inside a small fenced area, near the
end of a short grassy lane, is a low earthen mound on top of which is a U-
shaped setting of stones. Immediately beside this is a large stone slab
dotted with small 'cupmarks'. It is not at all clear what sort of ancient
monument this is but it gives the impression of something prehistoric,
maybe dating to the Bronze Age. Tradition has it, however, that the slab
formed the floor of the tent in which the future Saint Colum Cille was
brought into the world.

This Leac na Cumhadh or 'stone of the sorrows' is famous in the folk
beliefs of Donegal. In the past it was the practice of poor emigrants, who
thought they were leaving their homeland forever, to come and stay there
the night before their departure. They believed that, as Colum Cille himself was an exile, sleeping here on the spot where he was born would 'help
them to bear with lighter hearts the heavy burden of the exile's sorrow'.
Manus O'Donnell gives the story of the flagstone as he had heard it in the
sixteenth century. On the night before Colum Cille was born his mother
Eithne saw a beautiful youth who told her that there was a flagstone in
Lough Akibbon and that it should be brought to a place called Rath Cnó,
and there the saint would be born. The flagstone was found floating on
the lake and Eithne's family carried it to the place specified. When the
baby was delivered the stone opened a cross-shaped niche for him. Eithne
was also believed to have brought forth a round, blood-coloured stone, *an*

cloch ruadh – 'the red stone'. According to O'Donnell, Colum Cille left that stone in Gartan 'to work marvels and wonders, and it would not allow a covering of gold or silver for itself despite that such was often attempted but it did "suffer" a case of silver or of gold'.

Half a mile to the north, in the townland of Churchtown, is another site associated with the early life of the saint. Here the ruins of a small, six-teenth-century chapel survive and, nearby, are the badly preserved remains of two plain stone crosses, the foundations of a rectangular structure known as the 'Abbey' and a 'holy well'. A *turas* or a pilgrimage in honour of Colum Cille has been performed at this place from time immemorial and, even today, the little altar inside the ruined church is usually heaped with the trifle offerings of those who come to seek the assistance of the saint.

Another local tradition, which is still widely respected, is that the unusual, white 'Gartan Clay' is a powerful charm. A similar tradition regarding clay from Tory island is also preserved as part of Columban lore. In Tory it is the Ó Dúgáin family which has to extract the clay; at Gartan the same function must be performed by the O'Friels. Manus O'Donnell says that the place where Gartan Clay is found is where Eithne first felt 'the sickness of childbirth' and where she spilled some of her blood.

> Flour isn't whiter or finer than that clay and whoever eats it or carrys it with him is never burned or drowned. Nor shall he die without a priest. And every woman in the pangs of childbirth who eats it shall be helped. And whoever puts it on his tongue on the first day that he is seized by a fever will have no bitter taste in his mouth as long as the fever lasts. And it is its nature to heal every disease. But it must be one of the natives of Gartan that digs the clay for distribution, for it is said that once a stranger went to dig it but [the clay] fled from him and went into the heart of a tree or a great trunk nearby, and it was not found again in its own place until holy water was sprinkled there and the place was blessed.

The truth, of course, is that we don't know where Colum Cille was born. The earliest surviving evidence – that from his Life by Adomnán, writing about a century after his death – tells us simply, 'the holy Columba was born of noble parents having as his father Fedelmith, Fergus's son, and his mother, Eithne by name, whose father may be called in Latin "son of a ship", and in the Irish tongue *Mac-naue*.' Unfortunately, there is no historical source earlier than the twelfth century connecting Colum Cille with the Gartan area, with the possible exception of the explanation of the placename Cill mhic nEnáin – Kilmacrennan. One of the saint's sisters is said, in a source dating to about the beginning of the eighth century, to have been the mother of the sons of Enán – *mhic nEnáin* – after whom the place is named.

Even the year of Colum Cille's birth is not certain. Adomnán implies that he was seventy-six years of age when he died in the summer of 597. There is a consensus among those who have studied the fragmentary evidence that he was probably born in 521, although arguments can be made for 520 and 522. The various sets of annals, which are extremely unreliable as guides to events at this early period, record dates as diverse as 518, 519, 521 and 523. Late tradition claims that his birthday fell on 7 December. It was also believed that he was born on a Thursday, although 7 December did not fall on a Thursday in the year 521. There are many associations in folklore linking Colum Cille and Thursdays, especially in the Hebridean traditions. These may be related to the beliefs that he could offer special protection from thunder and lightning. In the Germanic and Scandinavian languages, although not in Gaelic, Thursday is the day of Thor the ruler of thunder. The earliest Gaelic and Columban traditions of the Hebrides were later overlain by those of the Norse settlers of the islands.

> Thursday of Columba benign,
> Day to send sheep on prosperity,
> Day to send cow on calf,
> Day to put web in the warp.
> Day to put coracle on the brine,
> Day to place the staff to the flag,
> Day to bear, day to die,
> Day to hunt the heights.
> Day to put horses in harness,
> Day to send herds to pasture,
> Day to make prayer efficacious,
> Day of my beloved, the Thurdsay.
>
> (trans. from *Gàidhlig*: Alexander Carmichael
> in the Carmina Gadelica)

Colum Cille's father, Fedelmith, was a grandson of the Conall who gave rise to the celebrated Donegal Cenél Conaill dynasty. The Cenél Conaill remained extremely influential in the north-west of Ireland and beyond for over a thousand years. Conall and his many brothers were said to have been sons of the legendary Niall of the Nine Hostages from whom were descended the politically powerful families collectively known as the Uí Néill. From the sixth century onwards the Uí Néill ruled over most of the northern half of Ireland. As well as their own individual local kingdoms, they shared among themselves the sacral, high-kingship of Tara, whose

primacy over all the kingdoms of Ireland was repeatedly asserted throughout the second half of the first millenium. The Uí Néill, and the Cenél
Conaill as part of them, were very powerful people. Colum Cille was born
into a vigorous and expansive aristocracy. In medieval times the O'Friel
family claimed the privilege of being the closest blood relatives of Colum
Cille, being descended according to their genealogies from Iogen or Eogain,
his brother.

There are various traditions about the origins of Eithne. Some say she
belonged to the Leinster people known as the Uí Bairrche, who lived in
what is now County Wexford. In the extreme south-east of that county, in
the barony of Bargy which takes its name from the Uí Bairrche, is the
ancient ecclesiastical site of Ardcolum. This unexpected dedication to a
saint from the opposite extreme of the country may be a reflection of the
belief about the birthplace of his mother. An alternative genealogical tradition links her to a population group that lived beside Lough Erne in
County Fermanagh.

The Irish Life of Colum Cille, written in the twelfth century, says that
Eithne belonged to the Corpraige of Leinster. An altogether more likely
origin, if we are to accept the cumulative traditions concerning the place
of the saint's birth and early childhood, says that Eithne belonged to the
Corbraige from the Fanad peninsula north of Gartan.[1] We know very little
about these people but they appear to have been a relatively unimportant
tribe which came to be dominated at the very beginning of the early
historic period, in the fifth or sixth century, by the expansion of the Cenél
Conaill. There is a tradition that Eithne is buried in Scotland, on the island
of Eileach an Naoimh in the Garvellachs, south of Mull. The spot is
marked by a small, circular enclosure, about three metres in diameter, with
a number of upright slabs, one of which has an incised cross.

We know something about other close members of Colum Cille's family from a list which appears to have been drawn up about the beginning
of the eighth century. This list was preserved among the records of the
cathedral at Durham in England where there was a devotion to Colum
Cille up to the later middle ages.[2] We are told that he had a younger
brother Iogen (Eogain ?) and three sisters: Cuimne the wife of Mac-decuil
whose four sons were Mernoc, Cascene, Meldal, and Bran who was buried
in Derry; Mincoleth mother of the sons of Enán, after whom the monastery of Kilmacrennan (Cill mhic nEnáin) near Gartan was named, and one
of whom was called Colmán; and Sinech, mother of the men of mocu-
Céin (probably the Cianachta from the valley of the River Roe in the
present County Derry), whose names were Aidan (a monk), and Conrí
(probably another monk) who was buried at the Columban monastery of
Durrow. Sinech was also the grandmother of To-chumme, a priest who
died in old age on Iona.

Ernán, who went with Colum Cille to Iona, was one of his uncles, probably on his mother's side. Another uncle, Brendan, was his father's brother, and his sons, Baithín (also called Conín) and Cobthach, first cousins of Colum Cille, were among those who left Ireland with him in 563.

The various Lives have stories in which the birth of this holy man is forecast. Many of the well-known saints, including the other two great 'patron saints' of Ireland, Patrick and Brigid, are said to have predicted his life. Adomnán records a number of these stories. In one of them, before the boy was born, his mother is said to have had a dream in which she was visited by an angel who gave her a marvellous, embroidered robe. The robe moved away but grew greater in size than the plains and the mountains and woods. Then the angel told Eithne not to grieve the loss of the robe as she would bear a son 'of such grace that he, as though one of the prophets of God, shall be counted in their number; and he has been predestined by God to be a leader of innumerable souls to the heavenly country'. As in many similar stories the description of the expansion of the robe is used retrospectively to suggest the foreknowledge of the growth of the influence of the saint. Two, almost identical, stories about the expansion of Colum Cille's own cloak occur in the folklore of Tory Island and Inishmore in the Aran Islands. Gort a' Chochaill, or the field of the cloak, is still pointed out on Inishmore.

Manus O'Donnell claimed that 'not alone was it the saints of Ireland and the patriarchs, who had the spirit of prophecy from God, that foretold the coming of Colum Cille but the druids and those that hadn't the faith foretold his birth a long time before it happened.' He instances as one example the story of Finn Mac Cumhail who loosed his famous dog Bran off after a deer at the stream at the head of Senglenn (the old glen) in southwest Donegal that was known in O'Donnell's time and to this day as Gleann Colm Chille. The hound refused to pursue the deer across the stream, something it was never known to have done before. Then Finn who was famous for his 'gift of knowledge' revealed the explanation. He said that Colum Cille would be born and that he would have many graces and much influence. He would come and bless the glen from the river and it would be a sanctuary for everyone that would go there for ever more. It was in honour of the holy man that Bran had mercy on the deer and did not pursue it across the stream. 'And from that time Belach Damhain [the path of the stag] is the name of the place where Bran spared the deer.'

A mile or so to the south of the Gartan area is the ancient church site of Templedouglas – Tulach Dubhglaise. Tradition says that it was here that Colum Cille was baptised into the Christian church and also where he took his first few walking steps as a baby. It is very unlikely that knowledge could have been preserved of where such ordinary events would have taken place in the early life of what, despite his undoubted aristocracy, was still a relatively ordinary boy. These beliefs testify more to a much later desire to provide real locations for the drama of the saint's life, and to associate already ancient sites in the landscape with an important local hero. Colum Cille appears frequently in the folklore of County Donegal. One of the characteristics of these stories is to associate him with very specific geographical locations and features which are still to be seen.[3]

Manus O'Donnell says that the boy was first given the name Crimthann, a word which means 'fox' or 'deceitful one'. However, 'the angels of heaven' inspired the other boys that played with him to call him Colum Cille, that is 'dove of the church'. This is the name by which he came to be known in Gaelic tradition in Ireland and Scotland, however, it is not at all clear that this was ever used during his own lifetime. Adomnán writing close to the year 700 always uses the Latin form Columba (literally 'dove'), as does Bede writing in 731. The poem written about 600 and later known as the *Amra Coluim Chille*, which is the earliest surviving text about him, refers to him only as Colum, although one line refers to a 'Columb ó Chille' – Colum of the church. Two poems written in Irish, apparently before 677 and maybe as early as the 640s, interchangeably use the names Colum and Colum Cille.

Many stories about the saint's childhood are preserved in the later Lives but our earliest historical evidence, much as we would expect, has actually very little to say about these years. Adomnán tells us that he was 'devoted even from boyhood to the Christian novitiate and the study of philosophy'. In another story Adomnán recounts how on one occasion the boy's foster-father, the priest Cruithnechán, saw a ball of fire above the sleeping child. Cruithnechán understood this as a sign of the special favour of the Holy Spirit. Fosterage or the sending away of children to be reared and socialised by another family was a common practice in early Ireland. However, fosterage with a priest must have been a fairly unusual practice and recognised as a form of novitiate. Colum Cille himself is said to have been the foster-father of Baithín, the man who succeeded him as second abbot of Iona. An amusing story in the Irish Life purports to tell how the commencement of his education came about. When Cruithnechán thought that the time was near he went to see a local seer (*fáith*) for confirmation. The seer scanned the heavens and told Cruithnechán to write out the alphabet for the boy. This was written on a loaf of bread which Colum Cille promptly ate, thus beginning his life of learning.

The later traditions claim that the place where he was fostered was Kilmacrennan, originally known as Doire Eithne, 'oakwood of Eithne' (his mother's name). The earliest church there seems to have been named in honour of the sons of Colum Cille's sister, Mincoleth. There is not much visible in the landscape today to remind us of what it might have been like

in the early sixth century. Sometime in the first few decades of the sixteenth century Manus O'Donnell, who composed the *Betha Colaim Chille*
and from 1537 was chieftain of the O'Donnells, built a friary here for the
Franciscans. The ruins of the friary's church still stand.

Just as with his childhood, tradition is rich with stories about Colum
Cille's days as a student and young cleric. Again our actual evidence is
very limited. Adomnán tells us that he spent at least some time while still
a deacon in Leinster studying with an 'old master' called Gemmán. In
some sources Gemmán was remembered as a Christian poet, a title which
suggests that he may have been a sort of Christian druid. We also know
from Adomnán that Colum Cille studied sacred scripture in Ireland with
a bishop called Findbarr who is often identified with the two saint Finnians,
respectively associated with the monasteries of Movilla in County Down
and Clonard in County Westmeath. There is no specific evidence to support either of these identifications and some scholars have argued that the
two 'saints' may actually represent just one historical person.[4] A lot of
confusion has arisen about the identity of Findbarr who is also referred to
by Adomnán by the alternative versions of his name, Vinniavus and Finnio.
These other names have a British Celtic (what we would now think of as a
Welsh) appearance to them, suggesting that either Findbarr was himself
British or that his name was for some reason remembered in a British
form. There were of course many connections between the Christian church
in Britain and that in Ireland in this early period. Patrick the 'apostle' of
Ireland was British. The oldest Irish 'penitential', or list of sins coupled
with their appropriate penances, is the penitential of Vinnian dating to
between 540 and 590. Some authors have suggested that this Vinnian
might be the Findbarr who was the teacher of Colum Cille.

We have to surmise that Colum Cille was ordained a priest as, strictly
speaking, this is not recorded in any contemporary or near contemporary
historical source. A late tradition claims that he was ordained by Etchen
said to have been a brother of the Cenél Conaill king, Aed mac Ainmerech.
This is extremely unlikely as both Etchen and Aed belonged to the generation following that of Colum Cille. In fact we have very little information about any of his activities before the year 563 when he left Ireland for
Scotland. Adomnán refers to him as 'the father and founder of monasteries'. Whether or not he was the founder of any monasteries in Ireland
before he left for Scotland is a major question. Bede says that 'before he
came to Britain, he had founded a noble monastery in Ireland known in
the Irish language as Dearmach, the "Plain of Oaks", because of the oak
forest in which it stands.' This is Durrow in County Offaly, but Bede's
version is contradicted by the words of Adomnán who implies that Durrow
was founded in the 580s.

The legends are quite definite that Colum Cille founded the monastery of Derry – his first and thus most loved monastery – before he left Ireland. The earliest version of this legend is found in the 10th or early 11th century preface to the Latin prayer/poem *Noli Pater Indulgere*, which claims to explain when, where and why the poem was composed by Colum Cille.

> Once at the time of king Aed mac Ainmerech, Colum Cille went to Derry to have a conference with him and there was offered to him the place with its appurtenance. At that time Colum Cille refused the place because Móbhí [abbot of Glasnevin] had prohibited him from accepting it until he should hear of [Móbhí's] death. But when Colum Cille came to the door of the place, there met him three of Móbhí's people who had with them Móbhí's girdle [as proof] and who told him that Móbhí had died.
>
> Colum Cille went back to the king and said 'The offer you made me early this morning, give it to me now.' 'It shall be given', said the king. Then the place was burnt with all that was in it. 'That is wasteful', said the king, 'for if it had not been burnt, there would be no want of garments or food there till Doomsday.' [But Colum Cille explained that everything would be alright]. Now the fire from its size threatened to burn the whole oakwood, and to protect it the hymn [*Noli Pater Indulgere*] was composed ... and it is sung against every fire and thunder from that time to this; and whosoever recites it at lying down and at rising up, it protects him against lightning flash, and it protects the nine persons of his household whom he chooses.[5]

The legend in its most developed form, as recounted by Manus O'Donnell, tells us that Colum Cille was studying at Saint Móbhí's monastery at Glasnevin, now on the outskirts of Dublin. The plague known as the Buidech connaill, 'Jaundice of the colour of stubble', broke out and the students were dispersed to their home territories for their own safety. Colum Cille went north to his homeland in Tír Conaill [Donegal] where the king, Aed mac Ainmerech, granted him one of his own fortresses at Daire Calgach [Derry] as the site for a monastery. Colum Cille first set fire to the place, in a form of exorcism to cleanse it of 'the works of worldly men that he might consecrate it to God and to himself'. When the fire grew too large the holy man pronounced the prayer *Noli Pater Indulgere*.[6]

> Father, keep under the tempest and thunder,
> Lest we should be shattered by Thy lightening's shafts scattered.
> Thy terrors while hearing, we listen still fearing,
> The resonant song of the bright angel throng,

As they wander and praise Thee, shouts of honour still raise Thee.
To the King ruling right, Jesus, lover and light.

(Trans. M. F. Cusack)

A scribe working in Derry in the twelfth century, and on very insub-
stantial grounds, went so far as, retrospectively, to give the date of 546 as
the year in which the foundation occurred. Colum Cille's church was said
to have been called the Dub Regles or 'Black Abbey'. A church of that
name certainly did exist in Derry from very early times because, when it
was burnt in a major fire in 1166, the annalists adds that this was something 'which had not been heard of from ancient times'.

However, despite a formidable ancient and modern tradition, historical
evidence does not support either such an early date for the foundation of
the monastery of Derry nor the attribution to Colum Cille. The legendary
version can be challenged on various grounds. No historical source sup-
ports the idea that Colum Cille was a student at Glasnevin or taught by
Móbhí. In fact other, admittedly equally late, tradition suggests that they
were both students of Saint Finnian of Clonard. Aed mac Ainmerech was
probably not born in 546 and certainly was not king, even of his own
dynasty the Cenél Conaill, before the death of his father in 569. More
persuasively, there is separate evidence that the monastery of Derry was
founded considerably later and by someone other than Colum Cille.

Twice, Adomnán relates the date of Colum Cille's departure from Ireland to two years after the battle of Cúl Dreimne. The battle was fought in
561 in the vicinity of the later Columban monastery at Drumcliff, near
Sligo. The battle of Cúl Dreimne was a significant encounter in which the
northern Uí Néill defeated their southern Uí Néill rivals led by the high-
king of Tara, Diarmait mac Cerbaill. The cause of the battle is not recorded in contemporary texts but the annalists do say that the northerners
gained the victory 'through the prayer of Colum Cille'. The Annals of
Tigernach adds that Diarmait had the benefit of an additional, exotic weapon
– a druidic protective 'fence' of some kind. Whatever the facts, the battle
seems to have been remembered as a conflict between the forces of Christianity on one side and those of pagan druidism on the other.

The battle gave rise to many legends; the best known of them tells how
Colum Cille himself was in a way responsible for it.[7] He was said to be
visiting Saint Finnian of Clonard when he discovered a manuscript of the
Psalms. Fearing that Finnian would refuse him permission to make another
copy of it, he began to do so secretly. Some of Finnian's followers saw what
was happening and reported to their master, but Finnian decided not to
intervene until the copy was completed. At the appropriate time he sent for
Colum Cille and argued that the transcript was now his property as he had
given no permission for it to be made. Colum Cille was infuriated and

referred the matter to Diarmait mac Cerbaill, the high-king at Tara. Diarmait found in favour of Finnian and uttered the famous judgement:

> *Le gach boin a boinín, le gach leabhar a leabhrán* – To every cow its calf [little cow], to every book its copy.

It is often claimed that this is one of the oldest references in history to the concept of copyright, although the story dates to much later than the reign of Diarmait mac Cerball.

Colum Cille, now doubly infuriated, promised to avenge what to him seemed like an unjust decision. At that time a son of the king of Connacht, Eochaid Tirmcharna, was a hostage at Tara. While playing hurley, the young prince accidentally killed a son of one of Diarmait's men. He fled to the sanctuary of Colum Cille, but Diarmait, contrary to all precedent, refused to recognise the holy man's authority. The youth was executed and Diarmait, fearing Colum Cille's revenge had him watched so that he could not leave Tara. However, the cleric escaped and made his way back to the land of his own people, Tír Conaill. His kin were not prepared to accept the insults to their illustrious relative and so prepared for battle. The northern Uí Néill, including Colum Cille's own people the Cenél Conaill, and the neighbouring dynasty, the closely-related Cenél nEógain, along with the forces of the king of Connacht, made an alliance against king Diarmait. The result was the battle of Cúl Dreimne.

These stories are, of course, fictional and the character of Colum Cille that comes out of them is very much at variance to that shown in the more historical sources. However, there has been considerable debate among historians as to whether or not Colum Cille had any role in the battle or in the events leading to it. Some later legendary material suggests that guilt for his alleged role in the death of those who fell in the battle was the cause of his going into exile in Scotland. Adomnán records the fact that a synod held at Tailtiu (Teltown near Kells in County Meath) excommunicated Colum Cille 'improperly as afterwards became known'. This gathering may have taken place in August 562, the year after the battle, on the occasion of the Oenach Tailteann, the great assembly held in honour of Tailtiu, the mother of the Celtic god Lugh. The latter's festival, Lughnasa, was held by our reckoning around the beginning of August.

Adomnán tells us that when Colum Cille came to the assembly, Saint Brendan, the founder of the monastery of Birr (in County Offaly), rose and greeted the holy man. He remonstrated with his clerical colleagues saying that he had seen a vision which clearly indicated that Colum Cille was greatly favoured by God and was predestined to be a great leader. The assembly withdrew its decision of excommunication and instead honoured Colum Cille. Adomnán does not tell us what the reason for their incorrect edict had been. Some modern writers who think that there might be some kernel of truth in the legends point out that the synod was held in the territory controlled by Diarmait mac Cerbaill. It is suggested that the king may have tried to persuade the clerics to take revenge on Colum Cille in return for whatever role, if any, he had played in the battle of Cúl Dreimne.

'Pilgrim for Christ'

In the second year after the battle of Cúl Dreimne, the forty-second year of his age, Columba sailed away from Ireland to Britain wishing to be a pilgrim for Christ.

Adomnán, *Vita Columbae*

Whether these events were related or not, shortly afterwards, in the year 563, Colum Cille with twelve companions set out from Ireland for Britain 'wishing to be a pilgrim for Christ'. This form of voluntary exile became known in the Irish church as 'white martyrdom'. The similarity between the number of monks that travelled with him and that of the original twelve apostles has occasionally aroused scepticism. But, as Richard Sharpe has pointed out, Colum Cille may have been consciously and deliberately imitating the model of Jesus and his close followers.

A list which survives in a text compiled about one hundred and fifty years later names the twelve individuals.[8] There was Baithín (also known as Conín) and Cobthach who were first cousins of Colum Cille on his father's side. Baithín would succeed him on his death in 597 as second abbot of Iona. For a time he had served as prior of the dependent monastery at the unidentified location of Hinba in the Hebrides. So also, but for no more than a few days, did Ernán an uncle of the saint (probably a brother of Eithne his mother) who was similarly part of the original voyage. There were at least two other distant Uí Néill relatives in the original party. Scandal son of Bressal son of Énna son of Niall belonged to the Cenél nÉnnae who were settled in east Donegal in the Raphoe area. Like Ernán, Scandal was probably one of the older men who accompanied Colum Cille, as he belonged to the generation of the latter's father. His people, the Cenél nÉnnae, never attained high political power and soon disappeared as a distinct royal dynasty.

The other Uí Néill relative was Cairnan son of Brandub son of Meilge. Cairnan's great-grandfather was Énna Boguine a son of the Conall Gulbain who gave his name to the Cenél Conaill. Also among those who sailed away with the saint was the monk Diormit, who is described as Colum Cille's attendant. Diormit would figure in many of the subsequent stories told about events on Iona. The others that travelled with Colum Cille are named as the brothers Rus and Féchno (whose father was called Ródan), Lugaid mocu Theimne, Echoid, Tochannu mocu fir-Chetea and Grillan.

Bede says that Colum Cille left Ireland 'to preach the word of God to the provinces of the Northern Picts', but Irish sources are divided as to whether he went as a form of penance or simply to find a 'desert' place for prayerful contemplation. Most modern historians, as indeed the earliest evidence, would emphasise the latter. Tradition has it that he and his companions left from Derry, sailing down Lough Foyle and across the northern channel. The legends make out of this departure one of the great dramas of the saint's life, indeed, of the history of Ireland. Later poets put words into the mouth of the saint.

> The great cry of the people of Derry
> Has shattered my heart into quarters.
> Derry of oaks we are leaving,
> Tearful with gloom and with sorrow,
> Leaving here broken-hearted,
> To go to the land of the strangers.

The medieval writers heaped image upon image, making all of nature lament Colum Cille's departure. 'Because of this, the seagulls and birds of Lough Foyle pursuing the boat on both sides were screaming and screeching for grief that Colum Cille was leaving Ireland.'

Again we have very little actual information about the details of this voyage. Despite the existence of a number of sites along the western shore of Lough Foyle which are pointed out as having connections with the story, we do not know where they left from nor, indeed, where they arrived. Fourteen hundred years later, in 1963, a group of thirteen Church of Ireland clergy and laymen 're-enacted' the voyage from Derry to Iona. Their thirty feet long, canvas boat was specially constructed for the voyage by Jim Boyd, a professional currach-builder from Carrickfin, County Donegal. The boat left Derry in the early afternoon of 4 June and arrived at Martyr's Bay, Iona, just after eleven o'clock in the morning eight days later. Each evening the crew landed and camped until the following morning. The currach was equipped with a one-hundred-and-twenty feet square, lug sail, but even when this was in use it was necessary to keep the six oars operating continually in order to maintain course. The boat can now be seen in the Harbour Museum in Derry, on the banks of the River Foyle from where it set out thirty-four years ago and from where it was believed that Colum Cille had originally left in 563.

It is not at all clear that Colum Cille and his companions went directly to Iona once they left Ireland. Most of Scotland at this time was divided between the Picts who had been settled there since late prehistoric times, at least, and the Gaelic-speaking Dál Riata whose ancestors had migrated from what is now County Antrim around the fourth or fifth centuries. They were closely related to the Dál Riata still remaining in Ireland. We cannot be certain that the territory of the Scottish Dál Riata extended as far north as Iona in 563, as it would do somewhat later. This uncertainty results in the confusion as to how the Irish monks acquired control of the island. A retrospective entry in the Irish annals says that it was given to them by Conall mac Comgall, the king of Dál Riata. However, Bede, who is not particularly reliable for this early period, says that it was granted to the monks by the Picts after they had been converted to Christianity. Adomnán makes no reference to the island being granted by anyone, although he does tell us that the saint made a visit to king Conall shortly after his arrival in Britain, presumably at his fortress at Dunadd in Argyll on the Scottish mainland. We don't know how long this visit lasted. Adomnán suggests that the Irish monks arrived in Britain in early June and some later tradition claims that they arrived on the ninth (coincidentally the date of Colum Cille's death).

Iona is a small island of about two thousand acres which lies less than a mile off its larger neighbour to the east, the Isle of Mull. Iona itself is about three miles in length, north to south, and about one-and-a-half miles at its widest. Much of the island is rocky, exposing its fossil-less, Precambrian geology. A large area of the island is over a hundred feet above sea level, while Dún Í at the northern end rises to over three hundred feet. Colum Cille's monastery was located on the eastern side of the island facing across the narrow sound towards Mull and the Scottish mainland. The western side is exposed to the open Atlantic, although it is here around the curving Camus Cúil an tSaimh, 'Bay at the Back of the Ocean', that the sandy, level *machair* area is located, where the monks and later inhabitants cultivated their crops. The weather was a constant hazard, as Adomnán frequently reminds us, and the Annals of Ulster records that 'a great windstorm on the sixteenth of the Kalends of October [16 September, 691] caused the drowning of some six of the community of Iona'.

The name Iona, although in use since the later middle ages, appears to be one of the great mistakes of history, arising from a misreading by some unknown medieval scribe of Adomnán's Latin *Iova insula,* in which an 'n' is incorrectly substituted for the original letter 'v'. The most ancient version that we have of the name of the island in Gaelic appears to have been *Í* or, as Bede gives it in Latin, *Hii.* There is no adequate explanation of the name but some sources suggest that it derives from an old Irish word for a yew tree, while much later stories claim that it is derived from the feminine pronoun used when the monks first saw the island from the sea and cried out 'I see it ['*i*', literally 'her']'. Coincidentally, Adomnán is at

pains in the prefatory material to his Life of the saint to point out that the
Hebrew form of the Latin name *Columba* is *Jona*, possibly pronounced
Iona.

Evidence from recent archaeological work proves that Iona was inhabited in prehistoric times as well as in the centuries before the foundation
of the monastery.[9] Very few traces of the earliest monastery survive to the
present above ground. It is certain that it was located on the gently slop-
ing plain on the eastern side of the island. The site is now dominated by
the restored Benedictine Abbey, founded about 1200. The constant rebuilding of the monastery and Abbey over the centuries has also damaged
much of the underlying archaeological deposits.

The monastery was surrounded by a *vallum* or 'boundary', some of the
earthworks of which still survive. Studies of this indicate that it enclosed
a rectangular-shaped space, about eight acres in extent. Until recently this
was considered to be problematic by archaeologists, as contemporary early
monasteries in Ireland were almost invariably circular or subcircular in
shape. However, the latest work on the *vallum* seems to demonstrate that
the enclosure is older than the monastery and that this abandoned structure was reused by Colum Cille and his monks. The evidence of oak and
ash trees recovered from the bottom of the enclosing ditch would seem to
indicate that some time, sufficient for the growth of such trees, had elapsed
since the previous occupiers had left the site. Although people had clearly
been living there at some stage in the past, the island was most likely
deserted when the Irish monks arrived, probably in the summer of 563.

Adomnán mentions several of the monastic buildings, of which the
most important was the church. This is likely to have been built in what
Bede called the 'Irish manner', that is of timber construction. The wood
would have had to be brought over from the Scottish mainland. The huts
where the monks worked and lived are mentioned, including a particular
hut where Colum Cille slept on the bare rock with a stone as a pillow.
Colum Cille had another hut, built on a rise overlooking the rest of the
monastery, where he wrote and worked on his books. At least some of
these huts were made of wattles. There was a guest-house and a larger
building which was possibly in use for communal dining. There may have
been a special scriptorium and a library. A recent study lists at least twenty-
five books which must have been available on Iona before the beginning of
the eighth century, quite apart from those that were written there.[10]

Various sheds and barns are referred to, some of which may have been
outside the main enclosure. There seems to have been a smithy for iron-
working and a disused millstone was used subsequently as the base for a
cross. Other crosses were later set up on sites connected with special
events in the saint's life such as the two erected to commemorate the death
of Ernán his uncle; one outside the shed where the old man fell and the

other closeby where the saint was standing at the time. Of course, there was also a monastic burial ground. Adomnán tells us that the first of the monks to die and be buried on Iona was a Briton – or perhaps a monk called Brito. However, there is no historical justification for the rather gruesome, folkloric story, told in the later sources, about the 'foundation sacrifice' of the monk Oran, whose voluntary death was said to have been needed in order to consecrate the ground.[11]

There is a late text known as the 'Rule of Colum Cille' but it is very unlikely that it derives from the saint's own period. Rather than making regulations for the life of a monastic community like that on Iona, the rule is addressed to a hermit such as Virgno, whom we hear of living that sort of life for twelve years at the beginning of the seventh century 'in the place of the anchorites, in Muirbolc Már,' on the island of Hinba.

> Be alone in a separate place near a chief monastery, if your con-science is not prepared to be in common with the crowd. Be al-ways naked in imitation of Christ and the Evangelist ... A few religious men to converse with you of God and his Testament; to visit you on days of solemnity; to strengthen you in the Testaments of God and the stories of the Scriptures ...[12]

The principal duty of the monks was the worship of God through partici-pation in the various liturgical observances, together with private medita-tion and prayer. Singing, especially of the Psalms, is mentioned repeatedly by Adomnán, including the 'miraculous' power of Colum Cille's own voice to be heard at great distances. Study and writing were also of great importance although possibly not for all members of the community. One modern translator of Adomnán's Life remarked that Colum Cille always seemed to be surrounded by books, inkhorn and vellum.[13] The monks had to provide for their own domestic needs, erecting the various buildings and cultivating the fields on the *machair*. Sheep, cattle and a pack-horse are mentioned by Adomnán as belonging to the monastery. There are numerous references to boats and boating. The monks themselves, their animals, visitors to the island and bulky building materials would have had to have been transported frequently from Mull or the Scottish main-land.

Besides Iona, Colum Cille and his monks established a number of dependent monasteries on some of the other islands in the Hebrides and on the adjacent west coast of Scotland. One of these was at a place called Campus- or Mag-Luinge (Soroby?) on the island of Tiree, where there were at least two further monasteries, Artchain and Bledach. There was a monastery on the unidentified island of Elena and another at Cella Diuni near Loch Awe on the mainland. A monastery which figures several times

in Adomnan's Life, and which was founded before 574, was at the unidentified place called Hinba. As well as the main monastery at Hinba, there
was a hermitage nearby, at a place called Muirbolc Már. Richard Sharpe
thinks that these places might have been on the conjoined islands of Colonsay
and Oransay to the south of Iona, although other authors have located
Hinba on Jura.[14]

Colum Cille and his monks travelled fairly widely among the western
islands and on the Scottish mainland, going to Skye and Eigg and
Ardnamurchan and, journeying to the other side of the highlands across
the Druim Alban or 'Spine of Britain', up the Great Glen, as far north as
Inverness. They also received many visitors from Ireland and elsewhere,
both on Iona and at some of the dependent monasteries.

Bede says that Colum Cille 'arrived in Britain in the ninth year of the
reign of the powerful Pictish king, Brude son of Maelchon; he converted
that people to the faith of Christ by his preaching and example.' Several
modern authors, however, have cast doubt on this assertion. We do know
that the monks of Iona in subsequent times played a major role in the
conversion of the Picts, but it is unlikely that much of this was achieved
during the lifetime of the saint. Adomnán confirms that Colum Cille
made a number of excursions into the territory of the Picts, and possibly
more than one visit to king Brude at his fortress near Inverness. Brude
may have been living at the fort of Craig Phadrig, which excavation has
shown to have been occupied in the sixth century.[15] Among the items
discussed by the king and Colum Cille was the safety of the monks as they
voyaged around the western isles. He specifically requested Brude to persuade the subject king of the Orkney Islands to guarantee the safety of the
missionary Cormac Uí Liatháin when he went there. As reported by
Adomnán, these visits, or visit, invariable became the occasions for a
contest between the Christian miracle-working abilities of the saint and
the pagan powers of the king's magician, Broichan. Colum Cille was, of
course, victorious in all these contests but Adomnán does not say that he
was rewarded with the conversion of the king. Colum Cille does not seem
to have been able to speak the Pictish language as, on a number of occasions, we hear of him preaching through an interpreter.

On one journey in the territory of the Picts Adomnán tells us that the
saint had to cross the river Ness. There then follows what is surely the
origin of the later stories about the Loch Ness monster. The 'monster', a
'water beast', attempted to attack one of Colum Cille's companions who
was swimming across the river. The saint ordered it to retreat and the man
was saved. A group of 'pagan barbarians' watching, one of whose number
had been killed by the beast, were so impressed by 'this miracle that they
themselves had seen, [that they] magnified the God of the Christians'.
Scholars have debated whether this episode in the Life could be derived

from a real event in which the 'monster' would have been a genuine sea animal such as a bearded seal or a walrus. Others have suggested that Adomnán may have drawn the inspiration from one of the literary models for his own work, the *Dialogi* by Sulpicious Severus, in which a similar story is told about Saint Martin of Tours.[16] A separate miracle story told by Adomnán parallels that claimed about Saint Patrick. Colum Cille is not credited with driving snakes off Iona, but shortly before he died he pronounced that 'all snake poisons will be powerless to harm either men or cattle on this island, so long as the inhabitants keep the commandments of Christ.'

As well as his contacts with the kings of Dál Riata and of the Picts, Adomnán tells one story which, incidentally, reveals Colum Cille's friendship with the Christian king of the Britons of Strathclyde, 'Roderc son of Tóthal, who reigned at the Rock of the Clyde'. Rhydderch, as he would have been known to his own people whom we would now call Welsh, ruled over a kingdom which stretched from the Clyde southwards to below Ayr. However, his fortress at Dumbarton, or Ail Cluaithe, was on a dramatic rock outcrop on the northern bank of the river, below Glasgow.

Adomnán gives very little chronological information about the events he describes in the Life, but it is possible to infer some dates from the details. Colum Cille is said to be in Ardnamurchan when travellers arrived from Ireland with news of the deaths of the two Cenél nEógain kings, Báetán and Eochaid, which the annals place in 572. When the king of Dál Riata, Conall mac Gomgaill, died in 574, his successor Aedán mac Gabráin came to Iona. Colum Cille, who had been on Hinba and who had experienced a number of visions of an angel of the Lord instructing him to 'ordain' Aedán as king, crossed over to Iona and there, according to Adomnán, performed the ceremony. Although the exact nature of the ceremony has been questioned, some scholars consider that this is the earliest recorded instance in European history of the Christian inauguration of a king.[17]

The annals say that in 575 Colum Cille and his relative, the Cenél Conaill high-king Aed mac Ainmerech, attended the meeting known as the Convention of Drum Ceat. This event has been shrouded in its own set of legends but we know that it was principally a conference between Aedán mac Gabráin and Aed mac Ainmerech. The meeting seems to have been designed to ensure the independence of Scottish Dál Riata from the control of Báetán mac Cairill, the powerful king who ruled Ulster east of the Bann, tying them closer into an alliance with Aed mac Ainmerech.[18] The alliance agreed between the two dynasties at Drum Ceat held solidly until the battle of Mag Roth (Moira in County Down) in the year 637.

Legendary sources, the oldest of which occurs in the early eleventh century introduction to the *Amra Coluim Cille*, say that three matters were discussed at the Convention of Drum Ceat. Besides the issue of Dál Riata, the subject of the holding as a hostage by king Aed mac Ainmerech of the son of the king of Osraige (effectively present day County Kilkenny), and the proposed expulsion of the poets of Ireland were also dealt with at this 'convention of the kings'. The legends say that it was argued that the poets should be expelled from the country on account of their almost universal greediness. This motif occurs in a number of other stories from ancient Ireland. If there is any basis in fact to it, it possibly reflects an uneasiness with some of the more pagan inheritance of the poets as heirs of the druids. The poets of the early historic period seem to have represented the survival of the pre-Christian Celtic tradition at its most extreme. Colum Cille, who is remembered in tradition himself as a poet, is said to have intervened on their behalf at Drum Ceat, saving them from the expected fate. As a result the leading poet, Dallán Forgaill, is said to have commenced the composition of the *Amra* or praise poem in the saint's honour. However, Colum Cille asked him to desist with the poem until he himself should be dead, accordingly it was not finished until after 597.

The most recent study of the introduction to the *Amra Coluim Cille*, shows that 'it is entirely a literary construct', written in 1007-8, and cannot be taken as an account of events in the late sixth century.[19] Scholars are agreed that the alliance between the Dál Riata and the Cenél Conaill, however, was a genuine result of the Convention. Whatever about any other issues that were discussed, it is extremely unlikely that this meeting took place as early as 575. Aed mac Ainmerech did not become high-king until 586. It is much more likely that, as Richard Sharpe has suggested, the Convention of Drum Ceat took place about the year 590 and that its purpose was the forging of a local alliance rather than the holding of the great national assembly indicated in the legends.

It is clear from the incidental stories that Adomnán tells us about the events surrounding the Convention that the meeting was held in a location in what is now County Derry. The ecclesiastical writer John Colgan said, in 1645, that local tradition in his day was very precise that the Convention of Drum Ceat had taken place at the Mullagh or Daisy Hill, a prominent rise in the landscape just outside the present town of Limavady. Even in Colgan's time, a celebration was held there each year on All Saints' Day to commemorate the great sixth-century gathering.[20] All Saints Day (1 November) coincides with the ancient festival of *Samain*, the beginning of the Celtic year. This would have been an appropriate occasion for the holding of assemblies and the making of alliances and agreements, but the evidence of Adomnán is that the Convention was held much earlier in the year. He describes a meeting between Colum Cille and Comgall, the founder of the monasteries of Bangor, County Down, and Camus on the lower Bann near Coleraine. The meeting took place 'on a fine summer day ... after the conference of the kings in Drum Ceat, when the blessed man was returning to the plains of the [northern] sea-coast'.

In the late sixth century the area around Limavady belonged to the people known as the Cianachta Glenn Geimhin, a relatively unimportant, subject kingdom. Their territory, which included much excellent farmland, stretched along the River Roe from the fortress at Dungiven to below their other great fortification which still survives near to the Mullagh and is known as the Rough Fort. Precisely why the Convention would have been held there is something of a mystery, but the traditional site, which might be said to have been at the time in neutral territory, is a level-topped mound which has a wonderful, commanding view of the surrounding countryside. The dynastic group to which both Colum Cille and Aed mac Ainmerech belonged, the Cenél Conaill, had acquired an interest in the ownership of the nearby territory of Magilligan after the famous battle of Móin Daire Lothair in 563. In addition, one of Colum Cille's sisters, Sinech, appears to have been the wife of a leading member of the Cianachta.[21]

Possibly sometime around the same date, perhaps while visiting Ireland for the Convention of Drum Ceat, Colum Cille may have had some role in the foundation of the monastery of Derry. Almost all surviving ancient tradition is certain that Derry was the first of the saint's foundations and the one dearest to his heart, but such stories are the product of the Derry propagandists of times much later than the sixth century. The Annals of the Four Masters, written in the seventeenth century and without any additional historical support, says that Derry was founded by Colum Cille in the year 535. This would have been impossible as the would-be cleric would have been at most fifteen years of age. The usually more reliable Annals of Ulster says that 'Derry of Colum Cille was founded' in 546, but does not name the founder. The use of the title 'Derry of Colum Cille', however, betrays the entry as a retrospective insert, as it is not used again in the annals until the twelfth century when we know that the source for what would become the Annals of Ulster was being kept in Derry.[22] The 546 entry is a late piece of twelfth-century propaganda inserted in the annals by those seeking to boost the fortunes of Derry through linking its foundation with the famous saint. In fact, there is no historical evidence of any kind that Colum Cille founded the monastery of Derry.

Almost certainly, another entry in the annals, which there is no reason to doubt, gives the true picture. In 620 Fiachrach mac Ciaráin mac Ainmerech mac Sétni died. In some of the sets of annals he is identified as 'the [other] founder of Derry'. Whatever this may mean, it is clear that an alternative interpretation to the official version has survived, accidentally. Although we do not know what age Fiachrach was when he died we may presume that his involvement in the foundation of Derry occurred thirty or forty years earlier, around the 580s or 590s. Fiachrach was a younger relative of Colum Cille and the nephew of the king, Aed mac Ainmerech, who is said in the legends to have given his fortress as the site for the new monastery. Although there is no evidence to support the contention, it may be that following his participation in the Convention at Drum Ceat Colum Cille came to Derry where he was involved along with Fiachrach in the foundation of the monastery. Adomnán mentions Derry on several occasions as a port for the journey between Ireland and Iona or Britain, and one story in the Life almost certainly implies that Colum Cille knew, at least, about the existence of a church with its graveyard in Derry before he died in 597.

But the saint's principal foundation in Ireland was clearly the monastery of Durrow (now in County Offaly) and not Derry as is claimed in the legends. Durrow or Dairmagh, like Derry, is another oak-tree name, and this may have contributed to confusion about the foundation stories of the northern monastery. Bede says that Durrow was founded before the saint left Ireland in 563. However, references to Durrow by Adomnán, who was closer to the event both in terms of time and relationship to those involved, seems to show that the foundation occurred much later. The Annals of Ulster records the death of Áed mac Brénainn, king of Tethbae in 589 and a note entered in the margin adds that 'it was he who granted Durrow to Colum Cille'. This date fits closely with a reference by Adomnán to Alither abbot of Clonmacnoise at the time that Durrow was founded. Alither became abbot in 585 and died in 599. Adomnán, who may have had his own particular connections with Durrow, records Colum Cille's close interest in the affairs of that monastery and his detailed knowledge of what was going on there.[23]

The only other Columban church mentioned by Adomnán is Drumhome in south Donegal, although it is not definite that it belonged to the confederation of the saint's churches during his own lifetime. Most of the other well-known Irish Columban churches were founded at much later dates, by those who belonged to the *familia* or community of Colum Cille. What is clear from Adomnán's account is that Colum Cille made several separate visits to Ireland subsequent to the foundation of Iona. The legendary sources, claiming that he had left as a penance, held that he had vowed never to return to Ireland again. However, as it was well known that he did return, the storytellers were forced to invent extraordinary explanations of this apparent breach of promise. Manus O'Donnell put it most succinctly.

> A wonder to tell but Colum Cille did go back to Ireland, he having promised when he was leaving that he would not set foot on Irish soil ever again nor look upon her men or women nor consume her

food or drink. But Colum Cille fulfilled his promise completely for he had a sod of Scottish soil under his feet all the time he was in Ireland and there was a cere-cloth [a waxed blindfold] over his eyes and his cap was over that again and the hood of his cowl was over that also. In that way he saw not an Irish man or woman just as he had promised. And he brought with him sufficient provisions so as not to have had to consume any of the food or drink of Ireland as long as he was there.

3

'The Fifth of the Ides of June':
Colum Cille's Death

'I commend to you, my children, these last words, that you shall
have among yourselves mutual and unfeigned charity, with peace.'
Colum Cille's words in Adomnán's *Vita Columbae*

In the second preface to the Life, Adomnán tells us that it is his intention
to describe his subject's 'holy way of life' and 'some instances of his
miracles'. The account is divided into three 'books' or parts: 'prophetic
revelations', 'divine miracles effected through him' and 'appearances of
angels, and certain manifestations of heavenly brightness above the man of
God'. Throughout, he is referred to as 'Sanctus Columba', holy or Saint
Columba.

Adomnán tells a story which occurred four years before the saint's
death. Two men, an Irishman named Lugne mocu-Blai and Pilu who was
a Saxon, were watching Colum Cille in his hut when they saw his face
light up with joy but then turn to sadness. After their pressurising of him,
the holy man explained the reasons for his change of expression. He said
that he had seen a vision in which angels were on their way to accompany
his soul to heaven but that God had changed his mind at the last moment
'answering in preference the prayers of many churches for me'. If the
story has any basis in fact, Colum Cille must have been ill or through
some kind of crisis, and the monks in all the churches associated with him
were praying for his recovery.

Adomnán concludes his Life with a chapter detailing the last days of
the saint, his death and the events surrounding his burial. One day, late in
the month of May 597, the seventy-six year old man was taken in a wagon
to visit the monks who were working in the western part of Iona. He told
the monks that at Easter, during the previous month, he had desired to
die but that he put off his departure from the world for a little longer so
as not to spoil the great Christian festival. The monks grew very sorrowful
on hearing this and Colum Cille attempted to comfort them. Then still
sitting in the wagon, he turned towards the east, facing into the interior of
the island, and blessed it and its inhabitants. He was then brought back to
the monastery.

On Sunday, a few days later, while attending mass the saint's face was seen to glow again with joy. Adomnán tells us that again he had seen an angel who had been sent to bring him to the Lord. On the following Saturday Colum Cille along with his devoted attendant, Diormit, went to a barn belonging to the monastery and blessed the building and the two heaps of grain there, thankful that his monks would have enough bread for a year in the event of his departure. Diormit grew sad at these words and Colum Cille confided to him that he would die later that night.

Leaving the barn, the holy man walked back towards the monastery but stopped about halfway to sit and rest for a while. As he sat there, a white horse which used to carry the milk vessels between the cow pasture and the monastery came up to him and put its head on the saint's bosom. Adomnán, betraying a very personal affection, says of this incident that the horse was 'inspired, as I believe, by God, before whom every living creature has understanding'. The horse began to mourn and his tears fell freely onto the saint's body. Diormit began to drive the horse away but Colum Cille stopped and admonished him, and instead blessed his 'servant', the horse.

He then went to the top of a small hill that overlooked the monastery and promising that Iona would be a place of special honour, he blessed it. He returned to his hut and began writing a copy of the psalter. When he reached the thirty-third Psalm and the verse 'But they that seek the Lord shall not want anything that is good' he stopped and said 'Let Baithín write what follows'. Afterwards he went to the church for the reading of the office of vespers. When this was finished the saint returned to his lodgings and lay down on the bare rock which was his sleeping place with his stone pillow. While lying down he communicated to his attendant Diormit his last instructions to his monastic brothers, including that they should have 'mutual and unfeigned charity, with peace' among themselves. These were to be his last recorded words.

He rested for another while but when the monastery bell sounded midnight he rose immediately and ran to the church, reaching it before the other monks. At the altar he sank down on his knees in prayer. As more of the monks arrived, Diormit and a few others saw the holy man illuminated by an 'angelic light' which quickly faded leaving them to grope for him in the darkness. On finding him, Diormit lifted the holy man's head onto his lap. The other monks arrived with lamps and, seeing their beloved abbot about to die, they started to weep. Colum Cille's face was filled with joy and Diormit raised the saint's right hand to help him bless his brothers. With this he 'breathed out his spirit' and the church resounded with the lamentations of his brother monks. It was the first few minutes of 9 June.

The office of matins was sung by the community and then they carried the body of their late abbot back to his lodging. Over the following three days and nights the funeral rites were observed. All the time these were being performed a storm 'of wind without rain' raged about the island. The sea was so rough that it was impossible for anyone to cross the narrow sound between Mull and Iona, so only Colum Cille's own 'family' of monks were present at the ceremonies just as he was said to have foretold. When the obsequies were ended the body was wrapped in fine cloths and laid to rest in the grave which had been prepared already. Once the burial of the holy man was completed the storm abated and the sea became calm once again. What was believed to have been his pillow-stone was subsequently erected beside the grave as a monument, and was still to be seen there in Adomnán's time. Adomnán also says that visions continued to be seen at his graveside after his death.

At the time that Colum Cille died it is said that various extraordinary visions were seen in Ireland. For example Ernéne mocu Fhir-róide, who was later buried in the Columban monastery at Drumhome in south Donegal, claimed to have seen such a manifestation. As a very old man he himself told Adomnán, who was at that time a young man, about what he had seen. On the night of 8/9 June, 597, Ernene along with other men was fishing on the river Finn in east Donegal. Suddenly the heavens were lit up. What seemed like a great pillar of fire appeared in the north-west and rose up into the sky illuminating the earth as if it was midday in high summer. The pillar pierced the sky and then darkness followed. Other fishermen at other parts of the river reported seeing the same sight.

The traditional site of Colum Cille's grave is still pointed out on Iona, but there is a lot of confusion in the medieval sources about the location of the saint's body. A legendary story telling how he came to be buried in Downpatrick, in the same grave as Saint Patrick and Saint Brigid, is narrated by Manus O'Donnell.

> Mandar son of the King of Lochlainn [Scandinavia] came with a warfleet to the monastery [of Iona] and plundered it and its graves, and tore up its tombs and lifted its coffins to search them for booty. And they took away with them the wooden coffin in which was the body of Colum Cille. And they thought it was a chest in which there was gold and silver or other treasures of the world, so they took it to their ship without opening it. But when they were out at sea they opened the coffin and finding only the body of a man they shut it again and cast it into the sea. And by God's miracle and the grace of the blessed body that was in it, the coffin did not stay still until it reached Downpatrick. And the abbot of Down went out one morning and saw the coffin that had been cast ashore by the sea. He opened it and found the body inside. And he recognised

that it was the body of Colum Cille. When he realised that, he kissed the holy body and gave glory and praise to God who had sent it to him. He washed it and then put it in the tomb where Patrick and Brigid already were.

The Norman chronicler, Giraldus Cambrensis, writing fairly close to the event, tells how in 1185 the bodies of the three saints, with Patrick in the middle, were found 'in a cave that had three sections'. John de Courcy, who had led the Normans into Ulster, was present at the time and 'took charge when these three noble treasures were, through divine revelation, found and translated'. A text known as the *Office of the Translation of the Relics of SS Patrick, Colum Cille and Brigid,* printed in various editions in the early seventeenth century, claims to give a detailed account of this incident.[24] Long before de Courcy came to Ireland Saint Malachy, who died in 1148, had 'miraculously identified' the site of the burials inside the cathedral in Downpatrick. After his arrival, de Courcy applied to Pope Urban III for permission to translate them, that is to move them honourably to a better location. The pope sent as a legate, Vivian, cardinal priest of Saint Stephen in Monte Caelio, and the translation took place appropriately on 9 June 1185. However, a totally different story is told in the native Irish sources as recorded in the Annals of the Four Masters for the year 1293.

It was revealed to Nicholas Mac Maeliosa, the successor of Patrick [Archbishop of Armagh] that the relics of Patrick, Colum Cille and Brigid were at Sabhall [two miles from Downpatrick]. They were exhumed by him and great wonders and miracles were afterwards worked by them. And after having been honourably covered, they were deposited in a shrine.

Stripped of their miraculous and propagandistic elements, there is no need to dismiss the historicity of these two separate accounts. Presumably the genuine discovery of someone's bones lies behind each of these descriptions.

Colum Cille was remembered in tradition as, *par excellence*, the poet saint. The story about his intervention on behalf of the professional poets of Ireland at the Convention of Drum Ceat celebrates this reputation, even if it dates to long after the time of the saint. It was believed that he himself had composed several Latin prayer/poems such as the *Noli Pater Indulgere*.[25] The litany-like, Latin poem, *Adiutor laborantium* (Helper of workers), is also attributed to him and its recent editors see no reason to deny this association. This short poem, which was 'lost' until recently, has twenty-five lines, all of which end with the syllable *'um'*. It is composed in the abecedarian form, in that each subsequent line begins with the next letter of the alphabet. The author, 'a little man trembling and most wretched, rowing through the infinite storm of this age', appeals to Christ to protect him.

Very ancient tradition also believed Colum Cille to have been the author of the well-known poem, *Altus Prosator* (Father most high):

> Ancient of days, father most high,
> Who art, and shall be, as the ages go by.
> With Christ and the Spirit, in glory supernal,
> Who art God evermore, unbegotten, eternal.
> We preach not three Gods, but the unity, One,
> The Father, the Spirit, and co-equal Son.
>   etc.
> Zeal-kindled fire the unjust shall destroy,
> Who deny the Lord Jesus, our hope and our joy.
> And the good shall be raised in the heavenly choir,
> As our merit and glory have made each one higher.
>
> (trans. M.F. Cusack)

This relatively long Latin poem is also abecedarian, with each new stanza beginning with the next letter of the alphabet. It is rhythmical and the line endings rhyme. It has been described as a 'kind of early "Paradise Lost" '. The author deliberates on the nature of God, supernatural beings, creation, the nature of the world, the final judgement and other similar, associated topics. Stories about the poem say that Colum Cille composed it in return for gifts sent to him by Pope Gregory the Great. Gregory, however, is said to have been critical of some of the theology of the poem, particularly the playing down of the Holy Trinity. Despite the ancient traditions surrounding it and the views of some modern writers, it would not be possible to prove that Colum Cille was the author, but its most recent editors suggest that it was composed by some Iona monk, before the end of the seventh century.

We have to be even more sceptical of the large collection of poems or verses in Irish which are attributed to the saint.[26] These often purport to express his views about the individual monasteries associated with him, or his thoughts on leaving Ireland. They are invariably more recent literary works, from as late as the eleventh and twelfth centuries, often composed with deliberate propaganda intentions on behalf of the places where they were composed.

> How rapid the speed of my currach,
> With its stern turned upon Derry;

> I am sad as I travel by water
> On my mission to raven-filled Scotland.
>
> Sad is the grey-green eye,
> That glances back upon Ireland;
> No more will it see in my lifetime,
> Her men nor their beautiful women.

We do know that writing formed an important part of the activities in the monastery on Iona. It is generally agreed now that the underlying record which forms the essential structure of the various collections of annals, from which the chronology of early Irish history up to about the 740s can be established, derives from documents kept at Iona from its earliest days, the so-called 'Iona Chronicle'.[27] In this sense it can be argued that, in some ways, the very idea of Irish 'history' – the factual recording of the country's past – is an Iona invention. Even Adomnán when writing his spiritual Life of Colum Cille is at pains, like any modern historian, to demonstrate for his readers the sources of information about his subject.

There is considerable debate still as to when these records began to be kept at Iona as a contemporary chronicle, some claiming that this began as early as the abbacy of Colum Cille himself while others would argue for a date in the early or middle of the seventh century. What is not in dispute is that, at very least from the earliest days of the monastery, notes were kept of specific events for future reference. Adomnán describes one such incident when Colcu mac Cellach was in Colum Cille's hut studying beside him. The holy man turned to Colcu and told him about the death at that moment of a chieftain from the latter's district. At once Colcu wrote down on a waxed tablet the date and hour at which he had heard this news and he was able to confirm the details when he later returned home. Whatever about the historicity of this story, it demonstrates the process by which the 'Iona Chronicle' evolved.

Adomnán mentions on a number of occasions that books and pages of books written in the hand of the saint had miraculous powers. Among those he mentions is a 'book of hymns for the week'. None of these manuscripts is known to have survived, despite the fact that several of the great illuminated Gospel books, such as the Book of Kells, were later claimed as having been made by the saint himself. However, one manuscript possibly is the work of Colum Cille. The *Cathach* is a copy of the Psalms, measuring about 9 inches by 6 inches, which has been dated by modern scholars to the end of the sixth or the beginning of the seventh century. It is the oldest, surviving Irish manuscript. The black ink, lettering of the *Cathach* is particularly beautiful, in an already developed 'Irish hand', while the initial letters at the beginning of each Psalm are sparingly, but brilliantly, decorated with motifs taken from the La Tène art of the Celtic Iron Age, and are often outlined with orange dots. Tradition has it that this was the Psalter which became the subject of the dispute between Colum Cille and Finnian, ultimately leading to the battle of Cúl Dreimne. A recent study has suggested that the *Cathach* is the apparently lost manuscript known as the *Soiscél Martain* or 'Gospel Book of Saint Martin', which was one of the great treasures of Derry in the twelfth century.[28] It is probably impossible to prove any of this but the possibility still remains that the *Cathach*, which is one of our most beautiful manuscripts and is certainly of roughly the appropriate date, might well be the work of one of our greatest saints.

The oldest surviving poem in the Irish language is the *Amra Coluim Cille* or 'eulogy' of the saint. Modern scholars date the very difficult language of the poem to about the year 600, which is in keeping with the tradition that it was composed by the chief poet, Dallán Forgaill, as a tribute shortly after Colum Cille's death.[29] It has been pointed out that, despite the fact that it is in the normal, native tradition of praise-poetry, the *Amra* is greatly influenced by Latin learning such as that it might have been composed by a cleric. In fact Dallán Forgaill was himself later revered as a saint. One line of this fairly long poem tells us that it was Aed who caused it to be made 'once the warrior [Colum Cille] should go to heaven'. This Aed was almost certainly Aed mac Ainmerech the powerful Cenél Conaill high-king who died himself in 598.

The poem heaps praises on the holy man but gives us virtually no biographical details about him.

> ... Colm rises into high heaven
> at the coming to him of the angel of God,
> – A beautiful attendance.
> He made a vigil of his life.
> Short was his time.
> Paltry his sustenance.
> Everywhere a pillar of learning.
> An authority in the strict books of the law.
> Light of the North,
> Who brightened the West
> And enflamed the East.
>   etc.

The poem celebrates Colum Cille as a Christian warrior and hero. It emphasises his secular and sacred learning, and his charity. It tells us that 'in terror of hell he went to Scotland'. According to the poem 'he protected a hundred churches' and 'his blessing quietened the lips of the fierce ones among the people of Tay [the Picts]'.

4

Successors of Colum Cille

> This we know for certain, that he left successors distinguished for
> their purity, their love of God and observance of monastic rule.
>
> Bede, *Historia Ecclesiastica*

When Colum Cille died he was succeeded as abbot of Iona by his first
cousin Baithín, whom he himself had named as his successor. This was to
set a pattern, with many of the subsequent abbots coming from the saint's
own kin-group, the Cenél Conaill.[30] Baithín had previously been superior
of the monastery of Mag Luinge on the island of Tiree and he also had a
prominent position at the unidentified monastery of Hinba, but had returned to Iona to be in close proximity to Colum Cille as the founder's
death approached. Baithín was not to survive his cousin for very long.
The records of the date of his death are confused. 600 is given in some
sources but, as Máire Herbert has shown, he may have died as early as 598.
His feast day (what was believed to be the day that he died) was commemorated on the same date as that of his master, 9 June. A Latin Life of
Baithín has survived. Although, in the form in which we have it, it is
almost certainly much later in date and contains not much more than a
series of conventional miracle stories, it may be that it preserves some
genuine memories of the second abbot. The name of the Donegal parish
of Taughboyne (Tech Baithín ?), just south of Derry, is said to retain the
memory of a dedication to him.

The third abbot of Iona was Laisrén. Feradach, Laisrén's father, was a
first cousin of Baithín and, hence, of Colum Cille. We know that Laisrén
had previously spent some time in Scotland as he appears in one incident
recorded by Adomnán when the saint was making a journey through the
district of Ardnamurchan on the mainland. However, on another occasion
we hear of Laisrén in a position of authority (possibly as abbot or prior) at
the monastery of Durrow in the midlands of Ireland. Colum Cille, on
Iona, is said to have been miraculously aware that Laisrén was overworking
the monks at Durrow and was greatly relieved when he ordered them to
rest. We know very little else about this man or about Iona and the other
Columban churches during his period of office. Laisrén died in 605 and
was succeeded as abbot of Iona by Virgno.

Unlike the two previous abbots, Virgno did not belong to the Cenél Conaill. In fact it is possible that he was British. In some sources he is described as Fergna Brit, and there is some other evidence that he was not Irish. Adomnán tells a story about Virgno when he was a young monk on Iona. One winter's night, while the other brothers slept, Virgno went to the church to pray. After about an hour Colum Cille entered the church bathed in an angelic light. The following day the abbot forbade Virgno to tell what he had seen until after he, Colum Cille, had died. Much later when Virgno himself had become the abbot of Iona, he told the story of that night to his sister's son, the priest Commán, who later told it to Adomnán.

In 617, during Virgno's period in office, the annals describe 'the burning of Donnán of Eigg on the fifteenth of the Kalends of May [17 April] with one hundred and fifty martyrs.' Eigg is a small island away to the north of Iona and the Ardnamurchan peninsula. We are unsure about the connections between the church on Eigg and the monastery on Iona. Adomnán mentions that, on at least one occasion before 597, Baithín, 'was detained on the island of Eigg by contrary winds'. We do not know if he was carrying out some sort of business there or simply sheltering from a storm. There is no adequate explanation for the martyrdom of Donnán, but the story indicates some of the dangers encountered by these 'pilgrim' monks. Donnán is said to have been Irish and a number of late sources, such as the Martyrology of Oengus, purport to give an account of his death.

> It was that Donnán who went to Colum Cille to seek him as a soul-friend. But Colum Cille said to him, 'I will not be a soul-friend to a community of red [blood] -martyrdom; for you will come to red-martyrdom and your brethren with you.' And so it happened.
>
> Donnán then went with his community to the Hebrides, and they set up their settlement there where the queen of the country had her sheep. The queen was told this. 'Kill them all', she said. But everyone said that this would not be a very good thing to do. However, they came to kill them. At that time the cleric was at mass. 'Leave us in peace until the mass is finished,' said Donnán. 'Leave them,' [the killers] said. And when [the mass] was ended every one of them was slain.

However, there are a number of references to clerics on Eigg in the eighth century, implying the continuation of some kind of church presence there.

In 620 the annals record the death of Fiachrach mac Ciaráin mac Ainmerech mac Sétni. Fiachrach was a member of the Cenél Conaill, a nephew of that dynasty's powerful high-king, Aed mac Ainmerech, and a distant cousin of Colum Cille. In some of the sets of annals he is further identified as the 'other' founder of the monastery of Derry. It is not clear if other in this context is intended to mean 'alternative' or 'in addition to'; the confusion results from what we might call subsequent 'interference' with the historical record. In later times, references to Fiachrach must have constituted an embarassment to those promoting what had become the official version of the story of the foundation of Derry.[31] There is no mention of him in the legendary stories about this event, which circulated from at least the middle of the tenth century. Despite the fact that, at minimum, he had played some significant role in the foundation of one of their most important monasteries, Fiachrach is not listed in the catalogue of (often extremely obscure) Cenél Conaill 'saints' preserved by the historians of that dynasty.

Although they preserve his name and the year of his death, neither the Annals of Ulster nor the Annals of the Four Masters, both of which ultimately derive from Cenél Conaill sources, record the additional information about who Fiachrach was or why he was important enough to have his death recorded. It is only by accident that these details were preserved in the various sets of annals compiled in the south of Ireland and in the midlands, away from the influence of the Derry propagandists of later times. It is very difficult to resist the conclusion that those to whom fell the responsibility of preserving the history of Derry, from about the tenth century onwards, were extremely reluctant to give Fiachrach credit for his contribution to the foundation of the monastery, whatever his role. Fiachrach is the great forgotten hero of Derry's history. The only actual historical, as opposed to circumstantial and legendary, evidence as to who was the founder of that monastery relates to Fiachrach and not to Colum Cille.

In the year following Fiachrach's death the Annals of Tigernach records the construction of a church on Tory island. The monastery of Tory, on the dramatic island off the coast of Tír Conaill, Colum Cille's homeland, was, at least in later times, closely associated with the confederation of Columban churches. Although there is no historical evidence that Colum Cille visited the island, the folklore of Tory, and the Cloghaneely area on the adjoining Donegal coastline, is full of stories relating to the saint.

Colum Cille and his brother saints, Beaglaoch, Dubhthach and Fionán, are said to have been on the hill, Cnoc na Naomh, above Machaire Rabhartaig where the ferry now leaves for the island. They agreed that whoever could throw their crozier to Tory would have the honour of converting its people. Beaglaoch's crozier fell on the mainland at the spot where he founded the church at Tullaghobegly, Dubhthach's reached Inishdooey – one of three small islands between Tory and the mainland, while Fionán's split a rock so that a waterfall, named Eas Fionán after him, gushed out. Nearby he is said to have founded the church at Ray, nowadays remarkable for the magnificent, twenty feet high, plain ringed cross there.

Colum Cille's crozier, of course, reached Tory and to him, therefore, fell the task of converting its pagan inhabitants.

It is not clear if the 621 reference is to a new monastery on the island or merely the reconstruction of an older one, as the 'slaughter' of Tory, whatever that implies, is previously recorded in 617. A little over a century later, in 733, the Annals of Ulster records that 'Dúngal son of Selbach profaned Tory when he forcibly removed Bruide from it'. The use of the word 'profaned' clearly demonstrates that it was the monastery there that was in question. Whoever Bruide was, his name suggests that he had a Pictish or British background and, if he was 'worth' abducting, he may have been from an aristocratic or even royal family. It is probable that his presence on Tory came about from its connections with Iona. We don't know who Dúngal was either but, as Richard Sharpe points out, he may have belonged to the Cenél nEógain who were at war with their traditional rivals, the Cenél Conaill, that same year.

Virgno died in 623 and was succeeded as abbot of Iona by Ségéne of whom a lot more is known. Ségéne belonged to the Cenél Conaill; in fact he was a son of a brother of Laisrén, the third abbot. Under Ségéne's guidance the network of Columban monasteries continued to expand. The annals say that he himself was responsible for the founding of the church on Lambay island off the coast of north County Dublin, in 635. Perhaps more importantly, Iona influence began to be extended to the north of England. Christianity had, of course, been introduced to what we now call England during the Roman period. Saint Patrick was a product of that church. However, with the departure of the Romans and the arrival of the Anglo-Saxons and the other pagan Germanic peoples, Christianity had retreated mainly to the British (Welsh) parts of the country.

In 597, the year that Colum Cille died, Pope Gregory I – Gregory the Great – had dispatched to England Saint Augustine who subsequently set up the archiepiscopal church at Canterbury. Although Augustine was a monk, as indeed was Pope Gregory himself, there were, nevertheless, various differences of practice between this 'Roman' church and the 'Celtic' traditions emanating from Ireland. Some of these differences, such as the manner in which the monks of the distinct traditions shaved their heads, were of relatively superficial importance but none was so controversial as the difference over the method of the calculation of the moveable feast of Easter. Pope Honorius (who had been elected in 625) wrote to the Irish on this matter warning them, 'not to imagine that their little community, isolated at the uttermost ends of the earth, had a wisdom exceeding that of all the churches, ancient and modern, throughout the world'.

A synod of the Irish church had been held at Mag Léne near the Columban monastery at Durrow, about the year 630. The outcome was that some of the leading churches in the southern half of Ireland accepted the universal or 'Roman' view. The northern churches, perhaps taking their lead from Iona, refused to change. An Irish delegation to examine the matter went to Rome in 631. They were there at Easter when their calculations differed from the local practice by a whole month. A bitter letter on the subject from a certain Cummian, which was written in 631-2 after this debacle, survives. One of those to whom it was addressed was Ségéne, abbot of Iona. Precisely who this Cummian was we do not know. Some have suggested that he was abbot of Durrow, although the most recent editors of the letter lean towards him being Cummíne Fota of the non-Columban monastery of Clonfert in County Galway.[32]

Cummian wrote his letter to try to encourage Ségéne to adopt the Roman practice on Easter. He is concerned that documents had been issued 'excommunicating, expelling from the church and anathematizing those who go against the canonical statutes of the four apostolic sees – Rome, Jerusalem, Antioch and Alexandria – when these agree on the unity of Easter.' He warns the church of Iona on acount of the influence it enjoys over others; 'for you are the heads and the eyes of the people, and if they are led into error because of your obstinacy you shall answer according to Ezechiel, for the blood of each soul to the strict judge.'

However, Ségéne was not persuaded and he appears to have been one of the churchmen who wrote to Pope Severinus about this matter and received a reply in 640 from the pope-elect, John IV, following the former's death. Bede has preserved large portions of this letter if not its entirety. It is addressed to eleven named clerics, including Ségéne 'and the other Irish teachers and abbots'. As well as dealing with the Easter question, the Pope inaccurately, as it happens, accused the Irish of reviving the long since dead, Pelagian heresy. 'We beg you, therefore, not to rake up the ashes of controversies long since burned out.' However, notwithstanding the intervention of the papacy, the church in the northern half of Ireland, and especially in Iona, continued with its own practice for calculating the date of Easter for at least another half century.

Cummian's letter was also addressed to Beccán 'the hermit'. This was almost certainly the Beccán associated with the Scottish island of Rum whose death is recorded in the annals in 677. If the two were the same, then Beccán of Rum must have been allied with those who were 'conservative' on the question of the dating of Easter and, although he was a hermit, he must also have been an important member of the Iona community. Again, he can almost certainly be identified with the Beccán mac Luigdech of the Cenél nEógain who was the author of two praise poems in Irish in honour of Colum Cille.[33] These relatively long poems, (i) *Fo réir Choluimb* ('Bound to Colum') and (ii) *To-fed andes* ('He brings northward'), repeat some of the themes of Dallán Forgaill's *Amra* but go further in developing the idea of Colum Cille as the protecting saint (trans. Clancy and Márkus).

Colum Cille, while I live,
will be my chant, till the grave's tryst;
in every risk I'll call him,
when I'll praise him with my full strength.

(from *For réir Choluimb*)

Leafy oak-tree, soul's protection, rock of safety,
the sun of monks, mighty ruler, Colum Cille.

(from *To-fed andes*)

Notwithstanding the Easter controversies, when Oswald became king
of Northumbria in 634, according to Bede, he invited the monks of Iona 'to
send a bishop to teach the Faith of Christ to himself and his people'.
Adomnán says of this, 'for up to that time all the land of the English was
shadowed by the darkness of heathenism and ignorance, excepting the
king Oswald himself, and twelve men who had been baptised with him,
while he was in exile among the Irish.' Oswald's father, who had been a
previous king of Northumbria, was defeated and died in battle in 616. His
sons fled to take refuge among the Dál Riata and Oswald spent some time
on Iona where he was baptised. Oswald defeated Cadwallon 'the most
powerful king of the Britons [Welsh]' in a battle in 634. He attributed his
victory to a vision of Saint Colum Cille which he had seen on the night
before the battle, but he may also have had more practical assistance from
the Dál Riata. The victory brought him back to power in Northumbria,
indeed, Adomnán grandiosely claims that 'afterwards he was ordained by
God as emperor of the whole of Britain.' On a subsequent occasion,
probably while on another visit to Iona, the king gave an account of the
vision to the abbot Ségéne in the presence of the monk, Failbe, who
himself would become abbot in 669. Failbe told the story to Adomnán.

Bede gives a full account of what happened when a missionary was
sent to Northumbria. At first a man of 'austere disposition' was sent but
he had no success and returned to Iona. He informed his superiors that he
had been unable to achieve anything with the Northumbrians 'because
they were an ungovernable people of an obstinate and barbarous tempera-
ment'. A conference on the matter was organised at Iona because, while it
was regretted that this first mission to the English had been unsuccessful,
the Columban monks still wished to meet the Northumbrian 'desire for
salvation'. One of those present, Aidan, spoke up and remonstrated with
his unsuccessful colleague about the latter's methods. Aidan said that the
example of the apostles should have been followed, and a more simple and
gentle approach to the pagans should have been adopted initially, before
leading them to 'the loftier precepts of Christ'. At this, all eyes in the

conference turned towards Aidan and everyone began to pay close attention to him. All agreed that here was a person fit for the task, so Aidan was consecrated a bishop and sent to king Oswald.

Oswald granted Lindisfarne, near his own fortress at Bamburgh, to Aidan when he arrived in 635. Lindisfarne is an island, cut off from the mainland twice each day by the rising tide. Bede is fullsome in his praise of Aidan, although he points out that Aidan was not a fluent English speaker and remarks on how delightful it was to see the king, who himself had a perfect command of the Irish language, translate for the bishop.

> From then on, day by day, many Irish arrived in Britain and preached the word of God with sincerity throughout all the territories under Oswald's rule, while those of them that were priests baptised those who were converted. Churches were built in many places and the people joyfully gathered to hear God's word, while the king generously gave lands and endowments for the foundation of monasteries, and the English nobles and commoners were instructed by their Irish teachers in the monastic way of life.

Although retaining his criticism of Aidan's Iona Easter calculation, Bede, nevertheless, extols the bishop's humility, friendliness and charity, his disinterest in worldly wealth and his devotion to the Scriptures. Fragments of a decorated, early seventh-century copy of the Gospels or New Testament, known by its catalogue reference as A.II.10, survives in the library of Durham Cathedral. This could have been brought by Aidan with him to Northumbria, or else made in the monastery of Lindisfarne shortly after its establishment.[34]

Aidan is said to have introduced the Northumbrians to the Irish practice of fasting on Wednesdays (*Céadaoine*, 'first fastday'), and Fridays (*Aoine*, 'fastday'), and when invited to dine with the king he himself would eat 'sparingly'. On one such occasion, at the feast of Easter when king and bishop were just about to eat from 'a silver dish of rich food', a servant came in to report that a crowd of needy people were sitting on the road outside begging alms of the king. The king immediately ordered the food which he was about to eat to be distributed and the silver dish broken up and distributed likewise. Aidan, who was sitting beside Oswald, is said to have been deeply moved and, taking the king's right hand, he said, 'May this hand never wither with age.' Bede goes on to tell us that this prayer was heard and that even when the king was subsequently killed in battle his arm remained uncorrupted. The arm was preserved as a relic in a silver casket at the church of Saint Peter in Bamburgh at the time that Bede was writing in 731.

Aidan died on 31 August 651. He was staying at one of the king's residences as was his practice as he moved around the country preaching. His remains were taken across to his monastery on Lindisfarne and buried in the monk's cemetery there. Much later, when a larger church dedicated to Saint Peter was erected on the island, Aidan's bones were translated there to an honourable place at the right hand side of the main altar. This church was built in 'the Irish manner' (not of stone but of hewn oak, thatched with reeds) by Aidan's successor, bishop Finán who also was sent from Iona, however, a later bishop from an English background removed the thatch and covered the roof and the walls with sheets of lead.

Many miracles were believed to have occurred through the intercession of Bishop Aidan. The Life of Saint Cuthbert, written by an anonymous monk from Lindisfarne about 699, tells us about a vision which that important English saint had as a young man on the night of the death of Aidan.

> Cuthbert, along with other shepherds, was tending his master's sheep in the hills above the River Leader. As usual, he was spending the night in vigil praying without cease, with great devotion and single-minded faith ... The heavens opened and he saw angels descending and ascending ... with the soul of a saint carried towards heaven in their hands ... a few days later [he] heard that news of the death of our holy bishop Aidan had been announced at the same time of the night that [he] had seen the vision.

Bede in his Life of Cuthbert, written about twenty years later, claims that this vision was instrumental in Cuthbert's decision to enter monastic life. He chose to enter the community of Melrose, now in the Scottish Borders, which had been founded around 640 by the monks of Lindisfarne; one of several such monasteries founded throughout Northumbria.

On a number of occasions Adomnán speaks about descriptions of incidents in the life of Colum Cille, or testimony to his spiritual influence, being given in the presence of the abbot Ségéne. This has led some authors to conclude that Ségéne made a systematic attempt to compile biographical material about the saint by collecting the memories, among others, of those older monks who had lived directly under Colum Cille's abbacy.[35] Ségéne was associated with Beccán the hermit who was probably the author of two poems about Colum Cille. In our oldest manuscript of Adomnán's Life, the scribe, Dorbéne, has inserted a quotation from another biographical work which otherwise does not survive. This is the *liber de virtutibus sancti Columbae*, the author of which was the monk Cummeneus albus.

Cumméne, as the Irish form of his name would be given, himself became abbot of Iona in 657 following in a distinguished family tradition. Both his uncle Ségéne and his great-uncle Laisrén had been abbots before him. The quotation used by Dorbéne refers to the battle of Mag Roth, which took place in 637, and goes on to talk about 'from that day to this'. The *liber de virtutibus sancti Columbae* was clearly written after 637, but how much later is not clear. Some authors have suggested that the work was written after its author had become abbot, but Máire Herbert has argued that it is more likely that it was composed while Cumméne was a young monk under the direction of his uncle Ségéne.

Ségéne died in 652 and was succeeded as abbot by Suibne moccu Urthri. He did not belong to the Cenél Conaill and little is known about him. He died in 657 and was followed as abbot by Cumméne. From around the time of Cumméne's accession to the abbacy, perhaps reflecting his own literary and historical interests, we begin to have much greater detail recorded in the so-called 'Iona Chronicle', the missing document which underlies all the early entries in the later sets of Irish annals. Cumméne made a visit to Ireland in 661 and seems to have spent a considerable length of time there, perhaps making a formal visitation of the monasteries of the Columban confederation.

It was during his abbacy that the Columban world experienced one of its greatest setbacks. This resulted from the coming to a head of the still-simmering controversy about the date of Easter. The Columban mission to Northumbria had been a tremendous success. So successful was the work of Bishop Aidan and his colleagues that one English author has written 'from the mid-seventh century onwards Northumbrian Christianity became profoundly imbued with the best aspirations of Irish monasticism. From the Tweed to the Solway, hermits with English names but authentically Irish spirituality brought a general shift in the values of society and gave to northern England its "Age of the Saints"'.[36]

When Oswald died in 642 he was succeeded as king by his brother Oswiu. Oswiu's daughter married Peada the son of the king of the Middle Angles following his conversion to Christianity. Peada was baptised by Finán, Aidan's successor at Lindisfarne, and brought back with him to his own kingdom four priests of whom one was the Irishman Diuma. Diuma was later consecrated Bishop of the Middle Saxons and Mercians by Finán. When Diuma died, he was succeeded by another Irishman, Ceollach. Soon afterwards Ceollach retired back to Iona and was replaced by an English bishop who, nevertheless, had been consecrated, as Bede tells us, by the 'Irish', almost certainly with Lindisfarne or Iona connections. Thus the influence of the Columban church continued to spread throughout England.

Bede tells us that Oswiu had nothing but praise for the Irish having been taught and baptised by Irish men and 'having a complete grasp of their language'. We are also told that while Aidan was still alive the differences about the date of Easter had been patiently tolerated by everyone out of love for the undoubted piety of their bishop. However, Oswiu had married a Kentish princess, Eanfled, who followed the 'Roman' practice. Bede tells us that the confusion was so great 'that Easter was sometimes kept twice in the one year, so that when the king had ended Lent and was keeping Easter, the queen and her attendants were still fasting and keeping Palm Sunday.' This was of more than liturgical and theoretical importance at a time when, for example, sexual relations between husband and wife were restricted during lent.[37]

The king's son, Alchfrid, had been educated by the monk Wilfrid who was trained in the 'Roman' practice. Alchfrid had attempted, without success, to wean the Irish monks away from their practice by offering them land for a monastery at Ripon. In 664 it was decided to hold a synod to resolve these matters once and for all. The synod was held at Whitby, at a monastery presided over by the abbess Hilda, who together with her community supported the Irish side. King Oswiu and Alchfrid were there as, of course, was bishop Colmán together with his clergy from Lindisfarne. Colmán was the successor of bishop Finán. A number of English clerics who favoured the 'Roman' practice were present but also a venerable bishop Cedd, bishop of the east Saxons, who, although an Englishman, had been ordained by the Irish and favoured the Irish system. Bishop Cedd acted as interpreter between the Irish and the English at the synod.

King Oswiu opened the proceedings, stressing the importance of unity. He stated that the task of the synod was to establish which was the 'truer tradition'. He called on Colmán, his own bishop, to explain the origin of the rites that he practised. Colmán spoke and defended the customs which he and his predecessors observed. He said that they derived their authority from Saint John, the beloved disciple and evangelist. Then Wilfrid spoke. He explained that the custom he practised was that observed in Rome, throughout Italy, Gaul, Africa, Asia, Egypt and Greece. He argued that his was the universal practice of the church and that 'the only people who contend against the whole world are these Irish and their partners in obstinacy the Picts and Britons, who inhabit only a portion of these the two uttermost islands of the ocean.' Technical arguments about the precise dating of Easter followed and then, finally, Wilfrid summed up, addressing Colmán directly:

> For although your Fathers were pious men, can you imagine that they, a few men in a corner of a remote island, are preferable to the universal church of Christ throughout the world. And even if your Columba – or, if I may say so, ours also – if he was the servant of Christ, if he was a saint who could perform miracles, can he take precedence over the most blessed Prince of the Apostles, to whom our Lord said: 'Thou art Peter, and upon this rock I will build my

church, and the gates of hell shall not prevail against it, and I
will give thee the keys of the kingdom of heaven.'

When Wilfrid had finished, the king asked Colmán if it was true that the
Lord had said these words to Peter. When Colmán replied, the king asked
again if similar authority had been given to Colum Cille. Colmán merely
said 'no'. With this the king indicated that he would not contradict Peter
who held the keys to heaven, lest when he himself should turn up there
'he who holds the keys has turned away'.

The matter was settled. Having had his views rejected, Colmán, together with his followers who included 'all the Irish whom he had gath-
ered together on the island of Lindisfarne and also about thirty men of
English race', returned to Iona and an Englishman, Tuda, took his place
as bishop at Lindisfarne. Ironically, Tuda had been trained and consecrated a bishop in the south of Ireland where the 'Roman' practices had
already been adopted. Colmán took away with him from Lindisfarne, as
relics, some of the founder bishop Aidan's bones. Some of Colmán's
monks remained at the island monastery under Eata, formerly abbot of the
daughter-house at Melrose, who was now appointed abbot of Lindisfarne.
Many years previously, Eata had been one of the twelve original English
boys to whom Aidan had taught the Christian faith when he first became a
bishop. Bede, who obviously rejoiced in the triumph of the 'Roman'
customs, nevertheless speaks well of the charity and piety of the Irish
monks. He says that so simple was their existence that when they left the
island 'there were very few buildings except the church; indeed, no more
than met the bare requirements of a seemly way of life.'

After spending some time on Iona, Colmán and his followers crossed
over to Ireland. In 668 the Annals of Ulster records 'the voyage of bishop
Colmán, with the relics of the saints to Inis Bó Finne [off the coast of
County Mayo], where he founded a church.' He is also credited with
founding a monastery later at the village of Mayo itself, on the mainland,
for the English monks who had followed him from Lindisfarne. His death,
as 'bishop of Inis Bó Finne' is recorded in 676.

According to Bede, the English monastery at Mayo separated at a later
date from the Columban confederation and practised its own rule. There
were many English monks there in the time that Bede was writing, about
731, and the annals for 732 record the death of Gerald, 'the pontiff [bishop?]
of Mag Eó na Saxan'.

A group of important manuscripts, which are thought to have originated in Lindisfarne somewhat later than Colmán's withdrawal but show-
ing undoubted contacts with the Columban world, still survives.[39] The
Durham Gospels is a manuscript measuring about 13½ inches by 10½
inches. It now consists of 108 folios but many of its pages are missing. It

was considerably damaged at some point in its history. It is close in style to the Book of Durrow and the so-called Echternach Gospels now preserved in Paris, a manuscript about 13 inches by 10 inches, comprising 223 folios. It is often claimed that the Echternach Gospels had connections with Lindisfarne but a recent study suggests links, based on the style of the script, with a source in the midlands of Ireland. The Lindisfarne Gospels containing 258 folios, each about 13½ by 9½ inches, is one of the greatest masterpieces of insular art. Between the original lines of the Latin Vulgate text written in majuscule script, there is a translation in Old English. A note written in the same hand tells us that the book was made by 'Eadfrith Bishop of the Lindisfarne church'. This was probably between 687 and 721 or, as George Henderson has argued, no later than 698 when he became bishop.

Like the Durham Gospels, the Lindisfarne Gospels was preserved in Durham Cathedral during the middle ages. In 875, fearing the Viking attacks, the monks of Lindisfarne moved to Chester-le-Street on the English mainland. From there they moved to Durham before the end of the tenth century, bringing with them their Columban traditions. Durham claimed to have bones and relics of 'Columkelle' as late as the fourteenth century. Other texts associated with Colum Cille were also preserved in Durham, such as the exemplar and so-called B manuscripts of Adomnán's Life of the saint, as well as the lists of his relatives and the monks who accompanied him to Iona.

Cumméne had been abbot of Iona throughout the course of the Easter controversy in Northumbria. We are not sure how the 'Irish' churches in England related to the mother foundation on Iona, certainly Cumméne himself does not seem to have got involved directly in the Easter dispute. However, one of the principal results of the Synod of Whitby was the loss of the monastery of Lindisfarne to the confederation of Columban churches, as well as the considerable reduction of Iona influence in the north of England. In 664, the year that the Synod met, the annals which were being compiled at Iona, record a series of strange natural phenomena. There was an eclipse of the sun about five o'clock in the afternoon of 1 May, 'and in the same summer the sky seemed to be on fire. The plague reached Ireland on the Kalends [1] of August.' This plague had devastating results throughout the country, continuing for about four years, but it does not seem to have effected Iona to any significant extent.

Cumméne died on 24 February 669 and was succeeded by Failbe, a distant cousin. As a young monk Failbe had been present at Iona when king Oswald came to visit. As abbot, he spent about three years (between 673 and 676) in Ireland. Although it is not explicitly recorded, he undoubtedly spent this time making a visitation of the Irish Columban churches as seemed to have become common practice for the abbots of Iona, helping to bind the Columban confederation together. In the year that he went to Ireland the annals record a fire at Mag Luinge. This must be the monastery of that name on the island of Tiree frequently referred to by Adomnán. Three years after returning from his long sojourn in Ireland, on 22 March 679, Failbe died.

5

Adomnán and the *Vita Columbae*

The ray of light, the flame, the precious stone, and brilliant lamp
... that is Saint Adomnán, that is the noble and holy priest, Adomnán.

Betha Adomnáin

Shortly after the death of Failbe, Adomnán, the author of the Life of
Colum Cille, became ninth abbot of Iona. Some authors have suggested
that during the 673-76 period his predecessor Failbe spent in Ireland,
Adomnán, who seems to have been still living there at the time, was
identified as suitable for the abbacy of the chief Columban monastery. A
Life of Adomnán himself, in the Irish language, was written in the middle
of the tenth century but gives us little biographical information about its
subject. The work has been shown to be more useful as a commentary on
the times in which it was written.[40]

The Annals of Ulster has an entry for Adomnán's birth at the year 624,
but when he died in 704 (a much more reliable entry) it says that he was
seventy-seven years of age. This would place his birth about 627. His
father was Ronán son of Tinne of the Cenél Conaill and his mother,
Ronnat, belonged to the Cenél nÉnnae, who inhabited the good lands of
east Donegal, south of Derry. His family appears to have been settled in
south Donegal in Tír Aedha (Tirhugh), although he is often associated
with the monastery of Raphoe in the territory of his mother's people.
Paradoxically, another Adomnán died as bishop of the monastery of Ráith
Maige Enaig, close to Raphoe, in 731. A story in the twelfth-century Irish
Life of Colum Cille tells how when he was a small boy the saint went with
his foster father, the priest Cruithnechán, and took part in the Christmas
ceremonies at Ráith Maige Enaig. The Life is not explicit but the suggestion is that the monastery there owed some sort of allegiance to the Columban
community at Derry, at least in the twelfth century.

Adomnán of Iona seems to have spent some time when young close to
or even at the monastery of Drumhome in south Donegal. It has also been
speculated that he spent some time at the monastery of Durrow. In reality,
we know virtually nothing about his life until he takes over the leadership
of the Columban church. He probably didn't go to Iona until the period
of Failbe's abbacy, when he would have been already well over forty years

of age but, wherever he pursued his preparation for the clerical life, the Life he wrote of Colum Cille shows that he must have studied a range of Latin texts, as well as the Scriptures and liturgical works.[41]

The first time we hear of Adomnán in the annals after his appointment to Iona is in 687. In that year he returned to Ireland bringing with him the sixty captives who had been held prisoners by Ecgfrith, king of Northumbria, since they had been captured in a raid on County Meath in 685. Ecgfrith died shortly after this raid and was succeeded by his half-brother, Aldfrith, whose relationship with the Irish had been very different

Aldfrith was the son of the former king Oswiu, who himself had spent some time as a fugitive among the Irish between the years 616 and 633. During that time Oswiu is said to have met Fína, the daughter of the Cenél nEógain high-king, Colmán Rímid. Aldfrith was their son, but he was considered illegitimate in England. Aldfrith also had an Irish name, Flann Fína, and knew the Irish language in which he was believed to have composed poetry.[42] James Clarence Mangan made a metrical version of one of the poems about Ireland, alleged to be by Aldfrith, from the unrhymed translation of John O'Donovan.

> I travelled its fruitful provinces round,
> And in every one of the five I found,
> Alike in church and in palace hall,
> Abundant apparel, and food for all.
>
> I found strict morals in age and youth,
> I found historians recording truth;
> The things I sing of in verse unsmooth,
> I found them all – I have written sooth.
> etc.

Although a Northumbrian prince, Aldfrith spent at least two periods of his life in Ireland or among the Irish, firstly as a baby and perhaps as a small boy, and later as an adult when he was a fugitive from his brother Ecgfrith. Bede tells us that he studied among the Irish as well as the English. Some late sources claim that he was a pupil of Adomnán; he certainly was a friend of the Columban monk. In the same year that Ecgfrith had taken his Irish captives, Aldfrith was actually staying at Iona.

In 686, Adomnán was sent as an ambassador to the newly installed King Aldfrith to seek the release of the previous King Ecgfrith's Irish prisoners. Adomnán must have been almost sixty years of age, if not older, when he undertook this arduous journey to Northumbria. In 687 he brought the prisoners back to Ireland. Two years later, he returned to Northumbria. While there, he visited the important monastery at Monkwearmouth/

Jarrow and saw its outstanding library. He discussed the Easter controversy there with the abbot Ceolfrith and may even have met, as a young monk, the yet to become famous Bede, who would later write about him. On one of his visits to Northumbria, Adomnán presented King Aldfrith with a copy of his book *De Locis Sanctis*.[43]

Adomnán's account of 'the holy places' was based on the descriptions given to him by a Gaulish bishop, Arculf, who had travelled to Jerusalem, and later found himself on Iona. Bede, who made his own version of Adomnán's work on this topic, described how the original book came to be written.

> After touring the Promised Land, Arculf travelled to Damascus, Constantinople, Alexandria and to many islands; but while returning home, his ship was forced by a violent storm on to the west coast of Britain. After many adventures, he went to see Christ's servant, Adomnán, who, recognising that he was learned in the Scriptures and was well acquainted with the Holy Places, was delighted to welcome him and even more to listen to him. Accordingly, [Adomnán] quickly wrote down everything of interest that Arculf said that he had seen at the Holy Places. By this means, he compiled a useful work for a great many, especially those who live far away from the places where the patriarchs and Apostles lived, and whose only source of information about them come from books.

It seems that on this second visit to Northumbria, Adomnán accepted (if he had not already done so before) the 'Roman' date for Easter, however, on returning to Iona he failed to convince his own monks. He may have been more sucessful in converting the Columban churches in the northern part of Ireland on some of his return journeys there. It was not until 716 that Iona would conform with the rest of the 'universal church' on this point.

In 692 the annals say that Adomnán visited Ireland. This was most likely a formal visitation of the Columban churches similar to that made on several occasions by his predecessors. He may have had to deal with the sort of problem adverted to by Tírechán who, when writing in the late seventh century, mentions the dispute between the communities of Colum Cille, of Armagh and of Eógan of Ardstraw, about the control of the monastery of Rath Cunga in south Donegal. Adomnán is likely to have returned to Iona for the following year when we are told that the king of the Picts, Brude mac Bile, was buried on the island. Two short, ironic verses commemorating this event are attributed, probably inaccurately, to Adomnán:[44]

Great wonders are worked
By the king born of Mary,
To Scuabán on Mull he gives life,
But death to Brude mac Bile.

It must be, at least, unexpected,
For him who was king of a *tuath* [tribal kingdom]
That an old, hollow trunk of an oak-tree
Should enclose him, the king of *Ail Cluaith*.

On less authoritative grounds, one of Brude's predecessors, Brude mac Maelchon the contemporary of Colum Cille, is also said to have been buried in Iona in 584.

Adomnán visited Ireland again in the spring of 697 to lead the Synod of Birr and, as the annals say, to give 'the Law of Innocents to the peoples.' The Law of Innocents, which was designed to protect clerics, women and children from combat and take them under the protection of Iona, eventually became known as Cáin Adomnáin, 'the Law of Adomnán', by which name it is referred to as 'a law of religion that inspires' in the secular law tract *Crith Gablach*. The original Law of Adomnán does not survive except in later expanded versions, however, a contemporary list of those said to be its guarantors, or those who agreed to enforce it, does survive.[45] The list includes leading churchmen and lay rulers from all parts of Ireland, and from both Dál Riata and the Pictish territories in Scotland. It also includes figures from both sides of the Easter dispute. The list is headed by the Cenél Conaill high-king of Tara, Loingsech mac Oengusso, a relative of Adomnán, who had come to power in the previous year. Adomnán's role at the synod is a clear indication of the prestige and eminence he had achieved in the Irish and Scottish churches.

As Máire Herbert pointed out, it is probably highly significant that the Law of Adomnán was proclaimed at a synod held in the year of the centenary of Colum Cille's death. Richard Sharpe draws attention to the story told by Adomnán about himself and his companions when they were returning to Iona from the synod. Having reached the unidentified Scottish island of Saine by 8 June, the eve of Saint Colum Cille's feastday, contrary winds forced them to halt their journey. They were anxious to be in Iona for the joyful festival. Adomnán prayed to his predecessor and, on rising at first light on the following day, found that the wind had dropped so that he and his companions could set out and sail back to Iona. They arrived about 9 a.m. and, having washed themselves, were ready to celebrate 'the holy ceremonies of the mass' at noon, in honour of Saints Colum Cille and Baithín. It was the one-hundredth anniversary of their founder's death.

We cannot be certain that the custom of specially commemorating centenaries was practised at this time, although it does seem likely as we know that anniversaries definitely were remembered. Adomnán must have also begun his other great work, the *Vita Columbae* or 'Life of Colm Cille', around this time. Whether this too was a conscious effort to commemorate the centenary of its subject's death is often debated. Certainly it must have been written close to the appropriate date as Adomnán himself died in the year 704.

In the Life, the author appears to collect all the evidence available to him about his subject from both written and oral sources. Unfortunately, from our point of view, he did not write a chronological biography. Frustratingly, he hints at topics we would like to know more about and avoids others we might consider to be of great importance. He may have deliberately ignored any evidence which cast his subject in a bad light. Instead, he compiled a work of hagiography to extoll the spirituality of his subject. This is set out in three sections or 'books' dealing with examples of Colum Cille's 'miraculous' powers, his 'prophetic foreknowledge' and his 'angelic visions'. He wrote the work at the request of his own monks but clearly also envisaged a wider readership. Writing in Latin and almost certainly tongue-in-cheek, he apologises in the preface for his necessary use of Irish language words and names, 'words that, I suppose, are held to be of no value, among other different tongues of foreign peoples'.

Some authors have stressed Adomnán's special interest in promoting the memory of his predecessor in Northumbria, following the loss of Columban influence there in the aftermath of the Easter controversy and the Synod of Whitby. He is said to have attempted to do this by placing Colum Cille on a par with the great saints of the church such as Martin of Tours, and even some of the leading apostles. One translator has gone so far as to describe the *Vita* as 'nothing less than the "Gospel of Colum Cille"' written principally for the Northumbrians.[46]

The oldest manuscript we have of the text of the *Vita Columbae* was transcribed by a cleric called Dorbéne, who asks us to pray for him in a little colophon or tailpiece attached to the end of the Life. He has been identified as the Dorbéne whose death as abbot of Iona, after only five months in office, is recorded by the Annals of Ulster on 28 October 713.

Dorbéne was another member of the Cenél Conaill, and thus a distant relative of Adomnán. He could have made his copy while Adomnán was still alive and even have shown it to the author before his death in 704. The manuscript, which consists of 68 pages of goatskin parchment, each almost 11 inches by 9 inches, is now preserved in the public library in the small town of Schaffhausen in Switzerland. It formerly belonged to the nearby monastery of Reichenau on an island in Lake Constance. Reichenau had many Irish connections in the early middle ages. Dorbéne's manuscript could have been taken there sometime in the eighth century. Three much later copies of Adomnán's *Vita*, the so-called B manuscripts, also survive. The best, B1, emanated in the late twelfth century from the scriptorium of Durham cathedral; the other two are clearly related to B1 in terms of their text. The B manuscripts preserve a slightly different version of Adomnán's original work to that of Dorbéne. The suggestion is that Dorbéne copied an early draft of the Life, whereas the B manuscripts represent a later version, possibly one corrected by Adomnán himself.

Another important Columban manuscript, possibly of around the same date as the Schaffhausen *Vita,* is the richly ornamented Book of Durrow which has 248 folios each about 9½ inches by 5½ inches.[47] The book contains a copy of Saint Jerome's Vulgate version of the four Gospels, together with some prefatory material. It is written in a beautiful, large, clear script known as Irish majuscule. The date and place of origin of the manuscript, like that of the Book of Kells, is still the subject of much scholarly debate. Between the years 877 and 916 the high-king of Tara, Flann mac Mael Sechnaill, had a somewhat too small *cumhdach* or box-shrine made for the book which caused a certain amount of damage to it. An additional note, entered in a blank space on the last page about the late eleventh or early twelfth century, makes it clear that the book was in the Durrow area at that time.

Around the beginning of the seventeenth century, the 'Book of Colum Cille', as it was by then called, was known to, and studied by, a number of antiquarians. Also, water in which the book had been dipped, or at least several pages from it, was known to local farmers in the Durrow area as a 'cure' for their sick cattle. In the later seventeenth century the book came into the possession of the library at Trinity College Dublin. It was there in 1689, when the college was temporarily occupied during the Williamite wars, that its *cumhdach* was lost.

Experts have argued for a long time about where and when the Book of Durrow was made; Northumbria, Iona, Derry, as well as Durrow itself, have all been suggested. What is common to each of these is that they were all part of, or considerably influenced by, Columban monasticism. The book shows some similarities to the fragments of a manuscript of the Gospels preserved in Durham, which is conventionally dated to about 650. Until recently many scholars accepted a late seventh-century date for the Book of Durrow, making it one of the earliest of the illuminated 'insular' Gospel books from Britain and Ireland. However, recent studies would suggest a slightly later date, in the early eighth century, about the time that Dorbéne was copying Adomnán's *Vita Columbae.*

Various other literary works are attributed to Adomnán.[48] While it is probable that he did write more than the two well-known works, it is also likely that those which are now associated with his name were written by other authors at much later dates. A set of dietary laws known as Adomnán's Canons list the animal foods which may or may not be eaten. A commentary on Virgil's *Bucolics* and *Georgics* is likewise attributed to him. The *Fís Adamnáin* is a text of about the eleventh century professing to describe a vision which Adomnán had at the time of the Synod of Birr. In fact it is a literary description of heaven and hell, perhaps composed by a cleric who belonged to the Columban community. A number of poems are also attributed to Adomnán, one of which, the *Féilire Adamnáin,* is a prayer addressed to all the saints whose festivals were celebrated throughout the year. The prayer of Saint Adomnán, a short poem of fifteen lines, is included in the eleventh-century *Liber Hymnorum.*

> Colum Cille,
> To God, please commend me
> When the time comes to die.
> May I not die too soon ...

Adomnán died in 704. His feastday (the day that he was believed to have 'gone to heaven') was commemorated on 23 September and, although he was almost certainly buried in Iona, a later tradition claimed that his relics were kept at Scrín Adamnáin, Skreen in County Sligo.

An early eighth-century collection of Irish church laws, known as the *Collectio Canonum Hibernensis*, is attributed to Ruben of Dairinis, who died in 725, and Cú Chuimne, a monk of Iona who died in 747. Cú Chuimne's death notice in the Annals of Ulster, which refers to him as '*sapiens* – the learned', has a little poem in Irish added in the margins of the manuscript, said to have been composed by his fostermother. The witty translation of the poem by John V. Kelleher picks up on the tradition that Cú Chuimne may not have always practised the highest ideals of monastic celibacy.[49]

> Cú Chuimne in youth
> Read his way through half the Truth.
> He let the other half lie
> While he gave women the try.
>
> Well for him in old age.
> He became a holy sage.
> He gave women the laugh.
> He read the other half.

The *Collectio* quotes, among others, from the writings of Adomnán. Cú Chuimne may have become a monk on Iona during Adomnán's abbacy, after he had renounced the sort of secular life referred to in the poem.[50]

The beautiful rhyming, Latin hymn, *Cantemus in omni die* (Let us sing every day), is said in the introduction to it in the *Liber Hymnorum* to have been composed by Cú Chuimne 'to praise the Virgin Mary in the time of Loingsech mac Oengusa [high-king of Tara, died 704] and of Adomnán ... The cause of its composition was to free [Cú Chuimne] from the evil life in which he lived, for he had a wife and lived a bad life with her.'

> *Cantemus in omni die*
> *concinentes varie*
> *conclamantes deo dignum*
> *ymnum sanctae Mariae*
>
> Let us sing every day,
> harmonising in turns,
> together proclaiming to God
> a hymn worthy of holy Mary.
> etc.

(trans. Clancy and Márkus)

There is some confusion in the sources regarding the succession to the abbacy of Iona in the years immediately following the death of Adomnán.[51] Some authors have suggested that this comes about because of internal controversy regarding the Easter issue. It may be that there were rival candidates for the office, some of whom supported the traditional Iona view and others who were more in tune with the 'Roman' position, that held by Adomnán himself. By 713 Dorbéne the scribe was abbot but, as his death notice records, he only held the position for five months. By 716, however, the Easter issue was settled. That year, the Annals of Ulster records that the date of 'Easter is changed in the monastery of Iona'. Bede tells us that 'the most reverend and holy father, Bishop Egbert, an Englishman, who had spent many years of exile in Ireland for love of Christ, and was most learned in the scriptures, and renowned for lifelong holiness came and corrected their error.'

Egbert was from an English noble background and as a young man he had gone to pursue religious studies in the south-east of Ireland, at the monastery of Rath Melsig. He spent most of his life in Ireland but near the end of his days he planned to go and preach to the German peoples. All his preparations had been made for the voyage and he had chosen his companions for the journey when he received a visit from a monk who told him about a vision he had seen in his dream which said that Egbert should go instead to 'instruct the monks of Columba'. The vision was repeated a few days later but Egbert still continued with his preparations for the voyage to Germany, however, a storm destroyed his ship. He finally accepted this as a sign that he was not to go to the Germans.

In 716 he went instead to Iona and persuaded the monks there to adopt the 'canonical rite of Easter and style of tonsure'. Bede describes what happened, using the opportunity to praise the Irish for bringing knowledge of Christ to the English and simultaneously condemn the Britons [the Welsh] for not being so generous with their knowledge.

> Being a very persuasive teacher who carefully practised what he taught, [Egbert] was listened to by all, and by his continual, pious preachings he drew them away from the obsolete traditions of their forefathers ... This occurred through a wonderful manifestation of God's grace, so that the nation which had willingly and generously laboured to pass on its own knowledge of God to the English nation might later, through that very same English nation, come to the correct knowledge which they had not previously possessed. In contrast the Britons, who had not shared their knowledge of Christ's Faith with the English, continue even now, when the English nation does believe, and is fully instructed in the teachings of the Catholic Faith, to be stubborn and crippled with error, going about with their heads incorrectly tonsured, and keeping Christ's ceremonies without unity with the Christian church.

Bede goes on to tell us that Egbert remained a further thirteen years on Iona and died there, paradoxically, on Easter Sunday [according to the Roman rite], 24 April 729. As Bede's text was written only two years later, in 731, we can be confident that he accurately recorded the dates of events which had happened so shortly before.

Notwithstanding the change-over to the correct calculation of Easter in 716, the following year the annals record 'the expusion of the community of Iona beyond the Dorsum Britanniae [the Spine of Britain or Grampian Mountains] by king Nechtan', the ruler of the Picts. This seems to mean that some of the Columban monks operating in the territories of the Picts were slow to change and hence were expelled by Nechtan who had his own direct lines of communication and information on this matter with the more orthodox church in Northumbria. It wasn't until the following year, 718, that the issue of the correct tonsure was settled at Iona. It appears that the conservative Irish tonsure required that the head be shaved from the forehead back, rather than in the approved 'Roman' manner in which the crown of the head was shaved.

According to the annals, in 727 'the relics of Adomnán [were] brought over to Ireland [from Iona] and the Law [of Adomnán was] promulgated anew'. Clearly even by that early date Adomnán himself was being treated as a saint. The relics were probably brought by Cilléne Droichtech of the southern Uí Néill, who had recently succeeded to the abbacy of Iona, and they may have been used to make peace between the Cenél Conaill and the Cenél nEógain who were at war that year. They remained in Ireland until 730 when, in the month of October, they were returned to Iona.

Sometime about 740 a copy of the document containing our earliest annalistic entries, the so-called 'Iona Chronicle', was brought to Ireland. It seems to have been taken to the famous monastery at Bangor in County Down. From then a new phase in Irish record-keeping commenced. Máire Herbert has suggested that, about the same time, a list of the abbots of Iona up to that point, together with their anniversary dates, may have been brought to Ireland likewise, which would later form the basis of the native martyrologies or 'calendars' of saints.

A similar origin may account for the list of Iona abbots preserved in the confraternity book of the abbey of Saint Peter in Salzburg. Around 742 an Irishman named Virgilius or Ferghil, who had almost certainly been a monk at Iona, went to Gaul and Bavaria. He was eventually put in charge of the diocese of Salzburg through his position of abbot at the monastery of Saint Peter there. He was properly consecrated as bishop in 755. A number of texts about him survive, including a letter from Pope Zachary which suggests that Virgilius was a believer in the heretical theory of the antipodes, 'that there are another world and other men under the earth'.[52] Colm Cille's cult was being spread to other ecclesiastical centres on the continent about this time through the circulation of versions of Adomnán's *Vita Columbae*.

Cilléne Droichtech continued as abbot of Iona until his death in 752 when he was succeeded by Slébéne of the Cenél Conaill. At some point during his term as abbot of Iona, Slébéne went to Ripon to examine the historical records of that monastery. The twelfth-century Life of Saint Kentigern, written by Jocelin of Furness (who also wrote a Life of Saint Patrick), records that a crozier of Colum Cille was preserved as a relic in Ripon. The story claims that Colum Cille went to visit Kentigern (who was also known as Mungo) at his monastery at Glasgow. 'Before bidding each other farewell they exchanged pastoral staves in pledge and testimony of their mutual love in Christ.' That stave or crozier was said to have been brought later to Ripon, which had been founded originally by Irish monks, but a more believable explanation might be that it was brought there direct from Iona as a gift by Slébéne.

In 753 the 'Law of Colum Cille' was enforced by the high-king of Tara, Domnall Mide. It may be relevant that in the following year, 754, Slébéne came on a visitation to Ireland. We don't know what aspect of life the Law of Colum Cille dealt with but presumably it must have been similar in type to the Law of Adomnán. Slébéne promulgated the Law of Colum Cille again in 757 and died sometime between then and 766 when his successor Suibne came on a visitation to Ireland.

Domnall Mide had come to power in 743. He belonged to the Clann Cholmáin of the southern Uí Néill, and in fact was the first of that dynasty to reign as high-king. As F.J. Byrne says, Domnall's reign of twenty years was extraordinarily peaceful, and the king himself was more than nominally Christian. On at least two occasions he retired to a monastery to enter 'clerical life'. One of these episodes occurred in 744, the year after his installation as high-king. As he was buried in Durrow on his death in 763, it is sometimes suggested that this was the monastery in which he had sought retreat earlier in his life.

There were clearly excellent relations at this time between the Clann Cholmáin dynasty and the community of Colum Cille, especially the monastery of Durrow. Domnall Mide's son, Donnchad who became high-king of Tara in 770, promulgated the Law of Colum Cille again in 778 along with the abbot of Iona, Bresal, who had come across to Ireland. On Donnchad's part, this may have been a sort of payment for the support of the community of Durrow when he fought 'a destructive battle' with the Munstermen two years earlier. The participation of Durrow in the battle is not too surprising. In 764 there had been a battle between the monasteries of Durrow and Clonmacnoise themselves, at an unidentified place called Argaman. We don't know the reason for the battle, but two hundred of the community of Durrow fell and Clonmacnoise had the victory.

6

Kells and the Other
Columban Monasteries in Ireland

Beloved are Durrow and Derry,
Beloved Raphoe without stain,
Beloved Drumhome of sweet acorns,
Beloved is Swords, as is Kells.

Attributed to Colum Cille

In 791, Artgal son of Cathal, king of Connacht, died in Iona. He must have
been on a pilgrimage or had retired there. Similarly, Niall Frossach, who
had been Cenél nEógain high-king of Tara until 770, died in Iona in 778.
Unfortunately, the close relations between the abbots of Iona and kings of
Tara received a set-back in 797. In that year Donnchad son of Domnall
Mide died, to be succeeded by Aed Oirdnide of the Cenél nEógain, whose
dynasty generally supported the aspirations of Armagh rather than the
churches of Colum Cille. Other matters were also bringing about changes
in Iona's fortunes. In 795, the island was attacked by Vikings as was the
Columban monastery on Lambay Island, just north of Dublin. In 802 Iona
was attacked again and burned, and, in 806, sixty-eight persons were killed
by these 'heathens'. Apparently, it was decided that something had to be
done.

A line from an eleventh-century poem, added in the margins of the
Annals of Ulster for the year 804, says that Kells in present day County
Meath 'was given without battle to the melodious Colum Cille [*Colum
Chille cheolach*] this year'. In 807 the annals record the 'building of the new
monastery of Colum Cille at Kells', and in 814 say that 'Cellach the abbot
of Iona, when the building of the church of Kells was finished, resigned the
office of superior, and Diarmait, the *alumnus* of Daigre, was appointed in
his place.' This has been taken to mean that Cellach retired from the office
of abbot of Iona and went to live in Kells which had been built as a sort of
refuge for the relics and the monks of Iona, its inland location safe from the
attacks of the Vikings. Kells [in Irish Cennanas] had been referred to in the
annals and other sources on many occasions prior to the construction of the
monastery there. Its traditions claim that it had been a royal site in prehistoric times.

It has often been asked why Kells was chosen as the site for this refuge from Iona. Surely if the traditions later claimed for it were correct, Derry would have been a more appropriate destination. But, despite tradition, it is unlikely that Colum Cille had very much connection with the foundation of the monastery of Derry. It was not his first monastery nor indeed the one 'most loved by him'. Such a tradition dates to a much later period than the life of the saint and, indeed we must assume, postdates the foundation of Kells. On the other hand Kells was located in Mide or 'Meath', the territory controlled by the southern Uí Néill kings who had been well disposed to the Columban community for most of the previous century.[53]

Kells is probably most famous because of its association with the Book of Kells, 'the most precious object in the western world' as the Annals of Ulster described it. The Book of Kells is the greatest of all the ornamented manuscripts from the early Christian period in these islands, an apotheosis, and one of the world's greatest artistic achievements.[54] Basically, it is an illustrated copy of the four Gospels. As we now have it there are 340 folios, each about thirteen inches by ten inches. We know that originally there must have been about thirty more folios which are now missing, and that these probably included some of the more elablorately decorated pages. The folios are made of vellum, the prepared skin of very young calves, approximately 180 of which were needed to make this one volume. These would have had to have come from a herd of about 1200 cattle.

The decoration of the manuscript was never completed by those who originally devised it. Although it is a consummate work of art, it neverthe-less contains several errors and corrections. In one instance a hole in the vellum has been patched and the writing continued across. We know that it is a collective work, although experts have differed about the precise number of contributers involved. It appears that four separate scribes, and two or three different painters or illuminators, worked on it, although some of the latter may have been reponsible for parts of the calligraphy as well. Attempts have been made in modern times to estimate how much work was involved in making such a complex artefact and it has been suggested that even one major illustration, such as the fabulously intricate *Chi Rho* page, would itself have taken as long as a month to produce.

The decorations and illustrations in the book draw on a number of the contemporary artistic traditions from these islands and beyond. There is a definite decorative and iconographic plan for the book, with an apparent emphasisis on eucharistic themes.

As with the other related manuscripts there has been a great deal of discussion about when and where the Book of Kells was made. We know that it was in Kells in its ornamented *cumhdach* or shrine when it was stolen in 1007. In the twelfth century it was used to record permanently some of the property transactions of the monastery of Kells. Early in the second half of the seventeenth century it was sent from Kells to Dublin 'for safety' and was subsequently acquired by the library of Trinity College.

Scholars disagree about the date of the book and this has a bearing on the place of its creation as the construction of the monastery of Kells does not seem to have been completed prior to 814. Most scholars would now seem to accept that the manuscript was made on Iona, conventionally around the year 800. Some have argued that it was made as a great display object, in effect an *hommage* in honour of the founder Saint Colum Cille, around the time of the second centenary of his death in 797. Parallels are often drawn between the illustrations in the book and the designs on the three magnificent high crosses on Iona: Saint Oran's Cross, Saint John's and Saint Martin's, which are said to have been completed, in the order listed, from the middle to the end of the eighth century. Two of the crosses, Saint Oran's and Saint Martin's, have depictions of the relatively rare subject of the Virgin and Child, as does the Book of Kells. The same theme is also alluded to in the eighth-century poem, *Cantemus in omni die* by the Iona monk Cú Chuimne. It is hardly coincidental that one of the very few depictions of this subject in Ireland is on the cross at the Columban monastery of Drumcliff in Sligo.

The foundation of Kells did not mean the end of the monastery on Iona, although it did continue to suffer at the hands of the Vikings. In 825 they attacked Iona and slew the abbot Blathmac and his companions because they had refused to reveal the hiding place of the valuable ornamental shrine which contained the relics of their founder. This story eventually reached Walafrid Strabo, a German cleric who lived between 808 and 849. In 838, he became abbot of the monastery at Reichenau, now in southern Germany, where there were Irish monks.[55] The library at Reichenau preserved Dorbéne's copy of Adomán's *Vita Columbae*. We don't know if the manuscript was there in Walafrid's time, although it is very likely. Walafrid was distinguished as a theologian and man of letters including poetry, and wrote various pieces of Irish interest, especially a Life of Saint Gall, and, in verse, the Life of Blathmac.

> A certain island lies off the Pictish shores, floating above the billowy sea; known as Iona, there the saint of the Lord, Columba, rests in the flesh ... The violent, cursed host ... approached the holy father [Blathmac], to force him to surrender the precious metals wherein lay the holy bones of Saint Columba; but the monks had removed the shrine from its stand and placed it in the ground, in a hollowed space under a thick sod ... In this way he became a martyr for Christ's name; and, as rumours testify, he is buried in that same place, and there many miracles occur on account of his holy merits.

The shrine was not discovered and was subsequently retrieved by the survivors of the raid, unlike the shrine of Adomnán which was stolen in 832, by the 'heathens', from Domnach Maigen, possibly Donaghmoyne in present day County Monaghan. There must have been more than one collection or container of the relics of Colum Cille as in 829 the new abbot of Iona, Diarmait, is said to have taken them back with him from Ireland to Scotland. Two years later he returned with them to Ireland. His successor, Indrechtach ua Finechta, also brought relics of Colum Cille to Ireland in 849.

That same year, Cinaed mac Ailpín united the Picts and Dál Riata into the kingdom of Scotland and moved his own residence from Argyll to the east of the country. He also transferred some of the relics of Colum Cille to the church of Dunkeld. This may have been on the basis of some agreed subdivision but, as Máire Herbert has said, the transfer inevitably involved damage to the influence and status of Iona. One of these relics may have been the crozier later known as the *Cathbuaidh*, 'victory in battle', which was carried 'successfully' as a talisman by the Scots in a battle against the Norse in 918. As George Henderson points out, the *Cathbuaidh* is shown along with other relics of Colum Cille on a thirteenth century seal of Dunkeld Cathedral chapter.[56]

In 854 Indrechtach 'the successor of Colum Cille [and] an excellent scholar suffered a violent death among the Saxons on 12 March'. The Annals of Innisfallen says that he was on his way to Rome. William of Malmesbury (1095–1143), the great Anglo-Norman chronicler, wrote a Life of a Saint Indract, the son of an Irish king who was murdered along with his companions near Glastonbury while returning from Rome. William had very little real data and, although it is almost certain that he was writing about the ninth-century abbot of Iona, he places the events in the late seventh and early eighth centuries. Indrechtach's successor, Cellach son of Ailill, died more peacefully somewhere in the territory of the Picts in 865. He was succeeded by Feradach son of Cormac who must have been responsible for the transfer to Ireland in 878 of more relics of Colum Cille, including the saint's 'shrine', 'which were taken in flight to escape the Vikings'. Feradach died in 880. He was succeeded by Flann son of Maíle Dúin of the Síl Lugdach branch of the Cenél Conaill, who died in 891.

Unprecedentedly, as Máire Herbert points out, Flann was succeeded as the *comarba* or 'successor' of Colum Cille, a title which seems to have come into use about the mid-ninth century, by Mael Brigte son of Tornán who had been *comarba* of Patrick, the title by which the abbot of Armagh was known, since 888. Mael Brigte who is afterwards styled *comarba* of Patrick and Colum Cille (his name and his title thus encompassing all three of Ireland's patron saints) belonged to the Cenél Conaill and died in 927. There is no evidence that he was ever in Iona. His appointment indicates that significant changes were occurring in the relationship between the Columban churches in Scotland and Ireland. The most obvious of these was that the position of successor of Colum Cille, previously reserved for the abbot of Iona, was no longer confined to the holder of that office. What did seem to be of continuing importance, although not always absolutely necessary, was the connection with the Cenél Conaill. A church and a cross dedicated to Colum Cille in Armagh, which are mentioned in the annals during the eleventh and twelfth centuries, may have originated at the time of Mael Brigte's joint abbacy.[57]

Despite these changes, Iona maintained its role as an important monastery. The deaths of its officials continue to be recorded in the annals, and it continued to be the burial place of kings from both Ireland and Scotland. Amlaíb, the Norse king of Dublin, ended his life 'in penintence' there in 980, having been converted to Christianity. This didn't prevent the monastery from being attacked by the Vikings on Christmas night, 986, when the abbot and fifteen of the most senior monks were slain. The island continued to be a destination for pilgrims. Mael Ruanaid Ua Mael Doraid, Cenél Conaill 'king of the North', went on pilgrimage to Rome in 1026, *en route* going first to Clonfert and from there to Iona. The death of the bishop of Stackallan in County Meath while on pilgrimage to Iona is recorded in 1047. The Lector of Kells, Maicnia ua hUchtáin, was drowned with others coming from Scotland (presumably Iona) to Ireland in 1034 with relics, including what was known as the *Cuilebad* or 'Colum Cille's fan'.

Mael Brigte son of Tornán died in 927. The next occasion when the title of *comarba* of Colum Cille occurs is at the death in 938 of Dubthach, a cousin of Mael Brigte, who is styled successor of Colum Cille and Adomnán. Máire Herbert has shown that Dubthach was the abbot of Kells. The title of *comarba* of Colum Cille, and the leadership of the Columban *familia* which went with it, had originated in Iona. It had passed, in effect, to Armagh under Mael Brigte and through him to Kells. It is not clear whether Dubthach was in Kells already or moved there on his appointment, although the inclusion of 'Adomnán' in his title might suggest that he had been associated previously with Raphoe or some other church especially connected with Adomnán.

Around this time a collection of the genealogies of fourteen Uí Néill successors of Colum Cille was compiled in Kells, using sources mainly derived from Iona. It would have been used to demonstrate the historical continuity of the successorship of the saint despite the change of location. It is also probable that some historical sources relating to Adomnán, compiled not too long after his death, were transferred to Kells around this time as well. Among them is the little verse in which Adomnán is said to speak about his own death on Iona.[58]

If on Iona death should come
That merciful end would be welcome.
No place under all the sky
Would be better than for there to die.

The ecclesiastical settlement at Kells had been developing by this stage, not just as a monastery, for a hundred and fifty years; it would continue to do so for another two centuries. Without excavation it has not been possible to identify the great subcircular enclosure, revealed in the present street pattern, with any particular phase in its earlier history, other than in a general sense. Likewise, it is still difficult to give precise dates for the high-crosses and early ecclesiastical buildings there. It is likely that the imposing Cross of Patrick and Columba (also known as the Tower or South Cross) at Kells is a monument to the linking of the two monastic communities in the person of Mael Brigte. This and other evidence would date it to the early tenth century, contemporary with the Market Cross. The other crosses, however, could date to the previous century. Ann Hamlin has suggested that some of the Columban churches such as Iona and Kells were pioneers in 'the development of free-standing stone crosses in the late 8th and 9th centuries.' A bell tower is mentioned in Kells in 1076 which is usually identified with the surviving Round Tower, but we cannot assign close dates to the small oratory known as Saint Columb's House.

In 904 Kells was 'profaned' when the Clann Cholmáin high-king of Tara, Flann son of Mael Sechnaill, attacked his own son, Donnchad, there, and 'many were beheaded around the oratory'. Donnchad, who would himself become king of Tara, seems to have been using Kells as a base from which to carry on a dispute with his father. In 920 Kells was attacked again, this time by the Vikings: 'the stone church was damaged... and a large number suffered violent death in it'. Again, in 951, Kells was attacked by the Norse led by Gothfrith son of Sitriuc from Dublin. The annals say that 'three thousand men or more were taken captive and a great spoil of cattle and horses and gold and silver was taken away'. The 'foreigners' then based themselves in Kells for a while, moving out to plunder other monasteries in the vicinity. Even if there is an element of exaggeration in this account, it is clear that Kells was a wealthy, busy settlement. It was attacked again in 969 and in 970. On the second occasion a large herd of cattle was captured. On both occasions the raiding Vikings were assisted by the Leinstermen.

The abbot Robartach, who had succeeded Dubthach and was also accorded the title of successor of Colum Cille and Adomnán, died in 954. He was succeeded by Dub-dúin of the Cenél nEógain whose family origins made his a somewhat unusual appointment. However, as Máire Herbert points out, the genealogists, perhaps tongue-in-cheek, defended his eligibility with the explanation that his ancestors had built a currach for Colum Cille. He died in 959.

Around this time the *Betha Adomnán* or Life of Adomnán in the Irish language was written. The modern editors of the Life, Máire Herbert and Pádraig Ó Riain, have shown that the work was composed at the monastery of Kells between the years 956 and 964.[59] Although it probably contains some basic material which does relate to its seventh-century subject, the *Betha* is, in effect, a *roman-à-clef* in which its author 'was presenting the events of his own time in terms of that of Adomnán'. In barely concealed historical fiction, the activities of Congalach son of Maíle Mithig, who became high-king of Tara in 944 and was assasinated in 956, are discussed and criticised. The stories told about the seventh century are parallelled with the events of the author's own time, and the hidden agenda of the Life is the retribution which will be suffered by kings who do not support the community of Colum Cille.

> [The] king of Tara ordered that the lands of Colum Cille should be on the same footing as the lands of [Saints] Patrick, Finnian and Ciarán as regards freedom from imposition. This, in effect, meant the [Columban] lands were declared subject to tribute. The matter was related to Adomnán who thought it unjust, for the men of Ireland had granted freedom of his lands to Colum Cille because he was of more noble descent than any other saint in Ireland. Adomnán said: 'Short will be the life of the king who gave the order. He will be killed by his own kin, none of his race will ever be ruler, and no one of his name will ever [again] be king of Tara.' And all of this came to pass.

The anonymous author was familiar with both secular and religious sources, including the annals and genealogies, and makes considerable use of the *Vita Martini* by Sulpicius Severus, just as Adomnán himself had done when he was writing his *Vita Columbae*. The Life is in the form of a homily for preaching on Adomnán's feastday, 23 September. It may be that visiting kings, and aspirant kings, were obliged to listen to it, sitting captive in a congregation for the solemn liturgies of the occasion. The Life points out that kings would disregard the saint and his community at their peril and that the family connections of their founder, Colum Cille, entitled his community to unquestioning support from the Uí Néill kings.

In 964 Mugrón succeeded as *comarba*. He was well known as a writer of verse.[60] A number of surviving works are attributed to him, among them a litany addressed to each of the three persons of the Holy Trinity and a traditional *lorica* or 'shield-poem' in which Christ's cross is invoked for protection. This poem is also sometimes attributed to Colum Cille himself. Another of Mugrón's works is a short poem in honour of the sixth-century saint. On his death in 980 the Annals of Ulster described Mugrón as the 'successor of Colum Cille both in Ireland and Scotland' and added that he 'ended a happy life'. A little verse about him *'comarba cadhlai Colaim'* is attached in the margin of the manuscript.

> Since God's son was born from heaven,
> Nine hundred years and eighty
> To the death of verse-praised Mugrón,
> Graceful heir of Colm.

In the year 989, 'Dub-dá-Leithe, successor of Patrick [since 965], took the successorship of Colum Cille by the counsel of the men of Ireland and Scotland.' The abbacies of Armagh and Kells were now joined together for the second time. Dub-dá-Leithe was about seventy-four years of age at the time, accordingly his appointment has been interpreted by some as semi-retirement from the Armagh position which, effectively, had made him head of the church in Ireland. Máire Herbert has noted that the *Liber Hymnorum* is a 'product of learned collaboration between the *literati* of the communities of Patrick and of Colum Cille in the period of monastic amalgamation', following the assumption of the role of *comarba* of Colum Cille by Dub-dá-Leithe in 989.[61] The *Liber Hymnorum* is an important anthology of early poems such as the *Noli Pater Indulgere* and the *Amra Coluim Cille*, supported by later explanatory material which purports to outline the circumstances of the original compositions.

Dub-dá-Leithe died early in the month of June 998 and was succeeded by Muiredach son of Críchán who had previously been a lector in Armagh. His appointment definitely indicates some kind of continuing link between the monastery of Kells and the church of Armagh, although the precise nature of this is not very clear. We know that the *familia* of Colum Cille was not a closed, separate institution in the sense of a medieval or modern religious order. Many of its officials, in Kells and elsewhere, also held joint positions in churches that were not closely associated with the Columban confederation. Muiredach held his post till 1007 when he retired, apparently, as the annals suggest to lead a more contemplative life. He died in 1011 and is given an elaborate death notice in the Annals of the Four Masters.

> Muiredach, son of Crichan, successor of Colum Cille and Adomnán, a learned man, bishop, and virgin, Lector of Armagh, and intended successor of Patrick, died after the seventy-fourth year of his age [the Annals of Ulster says eighty-fourth], on the fifth of the Kalends

of January [28 December], on Saturday night precisely; and he was buried with great honour and veneration in the great church of Armagh, before the altar.

In the year that Muiredach retired 'for the sake of God', the king of Tara, Mael Sechnaill who belonged to the Meath-based Clann Cholmáin dynasty, reconvened the ancient Fair of Tailtiu which had been in abeyance for nearly a century. Despite the antiquity of the kingship of Tara, a new all-Ireland power had arisen in the person of the Munster king, Brian Boru, who had cultivated relations with the leading church in the country, Armagh, as part of his national political strategy. Mael Sechnaill was forced to counteract the influence of Brian. At the Tailtiu assembly Ferdomnach was installed as the *comarba* of Colum Cille. Whether or not Muiredach was, as it were, pushed out to accommodate Ferdomnach, Máire Herbert believes that Mael Sechnaill was almost certainly acting to separate Kells from the influence of Armagh and its new patron Brian Boru.

Ferdomnach lived for only one more year but his appointment signalled the renewal of the former alliance between the southern Uí Néill and the *familia* of Colum Cille. Also in 1007, a year that saw several major changes there, the 'Great Gospel of Colum Cille', a manuscript which can almost certainly be identified with the Book of Kells, 'was wickedly stolen by night from the western sacristy in the great stone church of Kells. It was the most precious object of the western world on account of its human ornamentation.' The book was recovered two months later, hidden under a sod, but its gold decorations, probably mounted on its *cumhdach* or box-shrine, had been removed.

Kells was raided again in 1018, this time by Sitric and the Dublin Norse. The Annals of the Four Masters says that they 'carried off innumerable spoils and prisoners, and slew many persons in the middle of the church'. However, the settlement survived and recovered from the attack. From 1009, when Ferdomnach died, until 1040 the office of *comarba* was held by the Uí Uchtáin family. They also provided *fir léiginn* or 'lectors' to the monastery, one of whom may have been the author of the *Betha Adomnáin*. From around this time our sources of knowledge about the settlement become more detailed. Shortly before 1040 what are known as the 'Kells charters' began to be recorded, subsequently to be transcribed on to blank areas in the Book of Kells. These are mainly notes about the granting and transfer of land. They specify the names of many of the officials of the monastery and also demonstrate the ongoing relations with many of the secular rulers of the time, including the local Uí Mael Sechnaill kings and later the O'Rourkes from Breifne who begin to extend their influence to the Kells area from about 1117 onwards.

The annals continue to record the deaths of the *comarba* and incidents of more local interest. Burnings in Kells are recorded throughout the eleventh century. In 1060 the annals tell us that the settlement 'was completely burned, including its stone church'. Again in 1095 it was burned 'with its churches'. Many of these incidents, such as that in 1099 when it 'was destroyed by fire', were probably the result of nothing more sinister than accidents. But there were deliberate acts of violence by local lay people. In 1076 Murchadh son of Flann ua Mael Sechlainn, who had been king of Tara for only three nights, was killed in the tower at Kells.

Máire Herbert has drawn up lists of the occupants of the various offices of the monastery as recorded in the annals and 'charters'.[62] Besides the *comarba,* these include lectors, priests, resident superior/administrator, porter/sacristan, head of the hermitage, superior of the students, chief celebrant of the canonical hours, superior of the guest house and prior. Occasionally there is a mention of a bishop. There was a group of Céli Dé, or monks who followed a stricter religious discipline, attached to the monastery. These were housed in the *disert* and had their own superior.

Most of these offices were, in effect, hereditary and dominated by particular families. Many were heavily secularised. Belonging to the main community of the settlement, they were often involved in business and property transactions in which payments were made in gold and silver. In one case a priest acquires property for his sons. There was a market, and families of tradesmen. Kells also had a high reputation as a centre of learning. When Maelán the *Fer Léiginn* died in 1050 he is described as 'the most learned of all the Irish'.

By this stage the settlement had developed into a lot more than a monastery.[63] It was a 'township', with outlying agricultural estates. It had its own political life and was obliged to accommodate itself to external political upheavals, particularly in the first half of the twelfth century. Kells bore the brunt of the political struggles in the Irish midlands in the first half of the twelfth century – the time of the so-called 'high-kings with opposition' – when a number of individuals and dynasties from different parts of the country were attempting to establish a sovereignty over all of Ireland. During these struggles Kells was attacked and burnt on many occasions: in 1135, 1143, and three times in 1144.

Domnall mac Robartaig who succeeded to the abbacy in 1062 was almost certainly a son of a previous *comarba,* Robartach, who died in 1057, and a grandson of another *comarba,* Ferdomnach, who died in 1009. It seems that there was now a strong hereditary element in the succession to that office. The extent to which any of these individuals was in clerical orders has to be questioned; certainly they don't appear to have been constrained by celibacy. It was this Domnall mac Robartaig who was involved in the making of the great shrine of Colum Cille, later known as the *Cathach.*

In 1090 the Annals of Tigernach records that 'Colum Cille's reliquaries i.e. the Bell of the Kings and the *Cuilebad* [the fan] and the two Gospels, were brought out of Tír Conaill, together with seven score ounces of silver. And it was Óengus Ua Domnallán that brought them from the north.' Óengus is described in one of the Kells charters as 'the chief *anmchara* [soul-friend or confessor] of the community of Colum Cille'. He brought these precious items to the craft workshops of the Mac Aeda family in Kells to have them enshrined. The accompanying *largesse* of silver was almost certainly a gift from the Donegal king, Cathbarr Ua Domnaill.

The 'Bell of the Kings' is not easily identifiable, although some have suggested that it is the 'Bell of the Will' or Saint Patrick's bell which had its shrine made at the behest of Domnall Ua Lochlainn who died in Derry in 1121. Another suggestion is that it is the bell now known as the Bell of Saint Mura, associated with the monastery of Fahan about ten miles north of Derry. Although the latter bell is not known to have had any connection with the cult of Colum Cille, it is decorated in a style so close to that of the *Cathach*, and the similar object known as the *Misach*, that the work was almost certainly carried out by the same craftsmen.

In 1034 Maicnia ua hUchtáin, whose family held various positions of importance at the monastery of Kells, was drowned while crossing from Scotland to Ireland with the *Cuilebad* of Colum Cille which the annals say was lost also on the occasion. The *Cuilebad* was a *flabellum* or liturgical fan believed to be a relic of the saint. Either it was recovered, or a believable substitute was provided, because it too is listed among the items taken to Kells from Tír Conaill in 1090. The *Cuilebad* is mentioned in a version of the tale known as *Immram Snedgusa ocus Maic Ríagla*, 'the voyage of Snedgus and Mac Ríagal'. The tale occurs in various forms of differing dates, in both prose and verse. The fullest version is to be found with the title, *Sechrán clérech Choluim Cille*, 'the wanderings of Colum Cille's clerics', in Manus O'Donnell's sixteenth-century *Betha Colaim Chille*. There is another version dating to the eleventh century which purports to explain how the object came to be in Kells.

A local problem arose and an Irish king sent to Colum Cille for judgement. The two monks, Snedgus and Mac Ríagal, were dispatched from Iona with the decision. On their return, the wind blew them out into the ocean and, as in other early Irish voyage literature, they visited many islands where they encountered various wonders. On one island they came across a beautiful tree.

> And the bird gave a leaf of the leaves of that tree to the clerics, which was as large as the hide of a great ox; and told the clerics to take it with them, and place it on the altar of Colum Cille. And that

is the *Cuilebad* of Colm Cille at this day. And it is at Kells that it is.[64]

The *Cuilebad* does not survive and we have no exact idea of what it looked like. However, as Raghnall Ó Floinn suggests, some of the decoration on the early inscribed slabs in Glencolumbkille, or on the so-called 'Marigold Stone' in Carndonagh, may be based on similar types of liturgical instruments.[65]

One of the 'Gospels' mentioned in the 1090 list was almost certainly the *Cathach* – actually not a gospel but a copy of the Psalms – and the other may well have been the *Misach*. Although the *Misach* manuscript doesn't survive, the decoration of the box-shrine made for it is very similar in style to that of the *Cathach*. The *Misach* was originally associated with the cult of Saint Cairnech of Dulane in County Meath. However, a medieval text, *Aided Muirchertaigh Meic Erca*, 'the death of Muircertach mac Erca', parts of which may date to the eleventh century, says that the *Misach* along with the *Cathach* and the 'Bell of the Will' (better known as Saint Patrick's Bell) were given by Saint Cairnech to the Cenél Conaill and the Cenél nEógain.

The *Misach* was definitely in the Derry area in the middle of the twelfth century. We have only the merest outline of the process by which this came about. The Uí Uchtáin family who had held the abbacy of Kells from 1009 to 1040 had many connections with the monastery of Dulane. Presumably they transferred the *Misach* to the cult of Colum Cille at Kells and from there it was transferred to the north-west of Ireland, almost certainly to Derry, before the composition of the *Aided*. In the later middle ages the *Misach* was preserved by the O'Morrison family at Clonmany in Inishowen, County Donegal. It is now owned, appropriately enough, by Saint Columba's College, Rathfarnham, County Dublin.

The shrine of the *Cathach* consists of a small, hinged wooden box covered in decorated metal plates. As we have it now, some of the surface decoration dates to the fourteenth century and later, but the back of the shrine with its design of an openwork pattern of crosses, and the cast silver plates along the narrow sides, seem to be original. An inscription in Irish, which runs around three sides of the box, tells us about the making of the shrine.

> Pray for Cathbarr Ua Domnaill for whom this shrine was made and for Sitric son of Mac Aed who made it and for Domnall son of Robartach for whom it was made.

Cathbarr Ua Domnall was king of Síl Lugdach among the Cenél Conaill and from him would descend the O'Donnell chieftains of the later middle ages. The lands of Síl Lugdach were located in the north west of County Donegal and included within their territory Cloghaneely, Gartan, Kilmacrennan, Templedouglas and Tory, as well as other minor sites said to be associated with Colum Cille. The Síl Lugdach were clearly conscious of the Columban heritage which formed part of their patrimony. They had provided abbots to Iona and Derry in the ninth and tenth centuries. It may well be that the legend of Colum Cille's foundation of the monastery of Derry, as first outlined in the preface to the poem *Noli Pater Indulgere* dating to the tenth or early eleventh centuries, derives from a Síl Lugdach source.

Sitric, the maker of the shrine, belonged to a family which is recorded elsewhere as having been craftsmen in Kells. The Scandinavian origin of his first name is not too surprising. The foliage and zoomorphic motifs which are used to decorate those objects which have been identified as the work of Sitric or his associates show strong Scandinavian influences and parallels with artwork recovered from the Viking period excavations in Dublin.[66]

Domnal mac Robortaig retired as *comarba Coluim Cille* sometime before 1094 and died in 1098, perhaps, as Máire Herbert supposed, having travelled back to the north-west with the Columban relics including the *Cathach*. The history of that object in the twelfth century is somewhat obscure but it may have been one of the chief treasures kept in Derry, although not with that name. The Mac Robartaigh family, at least in later times, had lands close to Derry. There was another Mac Robartaigh family in south Donegal who were the keepers of the *Cathach* in later medieval times but we do not know what relationship, if any, existed between the two families. Neither do we know if there was any connection with the Ó Robhartaigh family who were associated in later medieval times with the Cloghaneely area of Donegal and nearby Tory Island, although such a relationship is likely given the Columban links of all these places.

In 1117 the abbot of Kells, Mael Brigte son of Ronán, was slain along with other members of his community by Aed Ua Ruairc and the Uí Briúin of Breifne on the eve of *Crom Duban* Sunday, at the beginning of August. The annalist was so appalled by this incident that he quoted Psalm 37 verse 17: 'The face of the Lord be against those committing these wickednesses, that he may wipe out their memory from the earth.' Aed's son, the famous Tigernán O'Rourke, came to power shortly afterwards and continued as an influential force in Irish affairs generally until his death in 1172. He is mentioned a number of times in the Kells 'charters', twice as a witness to the transactions of others and twice more as a granter of land himself. By that time the kingdom of Meath had disintegrated and the prestigious position of *comarba Coluim Cille* had been transferred to Derry.

Throughout the eighth, ninth, tenth and eleventh centuries, we continue to have reports of several of the other Irish monasteries associated with the traditions of Colum Cille. In addition to the more important centres there were, undoubtedly, many lesser churches which were connected with the cult of the saint, not to mention a wide variety of holy wells and landscape features scattered all over Ireland. Writing one hundred and fifty years ago, William Reeves, one of the greatest Columban scholars of all time, listed thirty seven *Sancti Columbae Ecclesiae Hibernicae* 'Irish churches of Saint Colum Cille', and in addition listed a further fifty-three in Scotland.[67]

One of the principal churches in Ireland was Raphoe in County Donegal where the memory of Adomnán, along with that of Colum Cille, was especially honoured. We have little precise information about this monastery. In 817 the Annals of Ulster tells us that Mael Dúin son of Cenn Faelad, the superior of Raphoe and 'a member of the *familia* of Colum Cille', was killed. The next entry says that 'Colum Cille's community went to Tara to excommunicate Aed.' Aed was the Cenél nEógain high-king, Aed Oirnide. F.J. Byrne thought that the killing of Mael Dúin may have been in retaliation for the death of Aed's brother, Colmán mac Niall, which was caused by the Cenél Conaill in 815.[68] 'Aed afterwards made an expedition against the Cenél Conaill.' In 959, the bishop of Raphoe, Oengus Ua Lapain, died.

Apart from the absence of historical records there are very few physical reminders of the monastery. Two fragments of a Romanesque period (12th century?) lintel-stone, depicting scenes from Christ's passion and crucifixion, are located at the present cathedral, which is likely to have been built on part of the monastic enclosure.[69] A Round Tower survived here until the early seventeenth century when it was removed by the Protestant bishop, John Leslie, for the construction of his new fortified palace. Interestingly, Bishop Leslie, like his predecessor, had previously been Bishop of the Isles, the Scottish diocese which included Iona. In 1635, King Charles I wrote to Bishop Leslie at Raphoe concerning a matter which originally had been the business of his predecessor.

> Reverend Father in God: Whereas we are informed that Andrew late Bishop of Raphoe at his transportation from the Bishopric of the Isles did without just cause or any warrant from our late royal father or us, carry with him two of the principal bells that were in Icolmkill [Iona] and place them in some of the churches of Raphoe; To which purpose we do remember that at the time of your being Bishop of the Isles you were a suitor to us for effectuating that thing at your predecessor the Bishop of Raphoe's hands which we now require of you: Therefore and in regard we have given order to the present Bishop of the Isles for repairing the cathedral church of

that bishopric [on Iona], and that it is fit for such things as do properly belong thereunto be restored; it is our pleasure that you cause deliver unto the said bishop these two bells for use of the said cathedral church with such timely convenience as may be; Which we will acknowledge as acceptable service done unto us.

Whitehall, 14 March 1635

The monastery of Rechru (Lambay Island) had been founded in the early seventh century and we have sporadic references to it in the annals throughout the eighth century. Tuathal son of Feradach was captured during a Viking attack on the island in 832 but survived. He may have been the son of the abbot, Feradach son Ségéne, who had died in 799. Tuathal himself died in 850 when he is described in the annals as abbot of Lambay and Durrow. There are other references to Rechru such as its burning in 795, when 'its shrines were broken and plundered', but it is difficult to distinguish these from references to Rathlin Island which had the same name, Rechru, in Irish.

Domnall Mide died, after twenty years as high-king at Tara in 763. During his reign he had many connections with the *familia* of Colum Cille. He was buried according to the Annals of the Four Masters in the monastery of Durrow 'with honour and veneration'. Interestingly the first two references to Durrow in the Annals of Ulster refer to the involvement of the community there in battles. In 764 the Battle of Argaman had been fought between the community of Clonmacnoise and the community of Durrow. In 776 the community of Durrow were the allies of the Clann Cholmáin in a battle against the Munstermen. On this occasion, unlike the first, they were on the victorious side.

In 833 Durrow was burned 'to the very door of [its] church' by the king of Cashel, Feidlimid, who had previously attacked and burned Clonmacnoise. In 836, during the first attack by the Vikings on the area of south Brega, 'Durrow of the Britons' as it is called (presumably on account of the numbers of students from Britain there) was plundered and many were killed, and many others taken away as captives. Sporadic references to the monastery continue through the ninth and into the tenth centuries. In 973 the superior of Durrow, Mael Muire, was drowned while crossing the River Erne at Assaroe. He must have been either coming from or going to the old homeland of Colum Cille in Tír Conaill, presumably on some kind of monastic business.

The deaths of several other officers of the monastery including superiors, scribes, a bishop and a lector are mentioned from the 9th to the 12th centuries. There are also references to the involvement of the settlement in local secular affairs. In 1019 the stone church of Durrow was 'broken down' by Muircertach ua Carraig in his pursuit of Mael Muad, the king of

Fir Chell. Mael Muad was forcibly taken from the church and put to
death. In 1095 Durrow 'with its books' was burned. The Leinstermen,
under their king Diarmait mac Máel na mBó, were defeated in Durrow in
1059 'through the miracles of God and Colum Cille'. In 1068, when
Donnchad son of Brian Boru was slain by the men of Tethba in revenge for
their having been plundered and preyed, 'his head was taken to Clonmacnoise
and his body to Durrow'. In 1137 there was another O'Brien connection.
Mór, the daughter of Muircertach O'Brien who was wife of the Ua
Maelsechnaill chieftain, 'died in Durrow of Colum Cille after penance'.
Murchadh Ua Maelsechnaill himself died in Durrow in 1153.

A finely carved Scripture Cross dating to the ninth or tenth century
survives at Durrow, together with a fragment of a second cross decorated
with interlace, and five early Christian grave-slabs. There may have been
a third cross also. The present church at the site may incorporate fragments of an early Christian period building, and, closeby, is the 'Head-
ache Stone' (actually the base of a high cross), and nearby again is 'Colum
Cille's Well'.

The monastery of Sord Coluim Cille (Swords, County Dublin), is first
mentioned in the annals in 965 when Ailill son of Maenach, bishop of
Swords and Lusk, died. The word *Sord* means a pure spring well. There
are many references in the annals to 'burnings' in Swords and to the
deaths of its officials throughout the eleventh and twelfth centuries. It was
to Swords, then as now on the main road to the north from Dublin, that
Brian Boru's body was taken after the Battle of Clontarf in 1014.

> Mael Muire son of Eochaid, successor of Patrick, with his venerable
> clerics and relics, came moreover to Swords of Colum Cille, and
> brought away the body of Brian, king of Ireland, and the body of his
> son Murchad, and the head of Conaing [heir designate of Munster]
> and the head of Mothla [king of the Déisi of Munster], and buried
> them in Armagh in a new tomb. For twelve nights the community
> of Patrick waked the bodies in honour of the dead king.

In 1035 the church at Ardbraccan in County Meath was plundered by
the Dublin Norse under their leader Sitric son of Olaf. The monastery of
Swords was plundered and burned in revenge by the Ua Maelsechnaill
chieftain. Clearly Swords was thought of at that time as belonging to the
Norse kingdom of Dublin.[70] In 1042, Eochagán, described as the superior
of Slane and the Lector of Swords and as 'a distinguished scribe,' died. A
student was killed by lightning there in 1056. In 1130 Swords was burned
again and many relics were destroyed. The only remains of the monastery
which survives to the present is the Round Tower with its pre-Romanesque
doorway.

The monastery at Drumcliff, now in County Sligo, was located in a strategic border location on the frontier between the territories of Cenél Conaill and Connacht. Apart from the Battle of Cúl Dreimne in the sixth century, two other important confrontations are recorded as having taken place near there: the Battle of Corann in 703 as well as a battle in 1012. Drumcliff is mentioned in the Annals of the Four Masters in 871 when the lord of Cenél Cairbre Mór was buried there 'under hazel crosses ...', and in the Annals of Ulster in 923 when its superior, who was also in charge of the monastery of Ardstraw in Tyrone, died. As with the other monasteries there are further casual references.

The main road from the west of Ireland to Donegal passes through the middle of the ancient monastic enclosure. A stump of a round tower is preserved, as well as the shaft of a tall, plain stone cross. A Scripture Cross, of about the end of the ninth or beginning of the tenth century, also survives intact. Like its sister crosses at the principal Columban monastery in Iona, the cross at Drumcliff has a rare depiction of the Virgin and Child.[71] Two fragments of a third cross from Drumcliff are now in the National Museum of Ireland. W.B. Yeats' grandfather was vicar at the church here, and the poet is buried in the graveyard which occupies part of the area of the ancient monastery.

Moone in County Kildare was another Columban church of some significance, if the magnificent, seventeen feet tall Scripture Cross there is any indication. For many people this unusually slender sculpture is one of the most attractive stone crosses of the whole Irish series. Its naive animal and human figures, depicting scenes from both the Old and New Testament, are frequently reproduced. Fragments of a second cross are preserved on the site also. There are early references to a *Eó Mugna*, said to have been a great, miraculous oak which grew nearby, and which was later given a Christian symbolism.[72] Máire Herbert points out that the earliest reference to the monastery, Móin Choluim, occurs in the early tenth-century text, the *Vita Tripartita*.[73] There are only a few perfunctory references to Moone in the annals.

There are many other notices, scattered throughout the annals, to churches and sites with Columban associations. In addition, a large body of literary texts most of which seem to date to the eleventh or twelfth centuries mention Colum Cille and the places in Ireland connected with him.[74] In 1041 Soerghus, the lector and *airchinneach*, 'monastic steward', of Tory died. The shrine of Colum Cille was stolen by the Norse of Dublin in 1127 but 'was restored again to its house at the end of a month'. The 'house' in question may have been the church of Scrín Coluim Cille in County Meath. The 'house of Colum Cille' at Kilmacrennan was taken by Ua Tairchert from Aed mac Cathbarr Ua Domhnaill in 1129, and 'it was burned over him'.

The monastery of Iona also continued to function throughout this period, with its abbot apparently retaining the title of *comarba Coluim Cille* until the beginning of the tenth century. The monastery suffered a number of major blows in the first phase of the Viking raids on these islands, and there were a number of similar incidents much later. However, as the ninth century unfolded and the Norse colonists began to settle in the Hebrides, *na hInnse Gall* (the islands of the foreigners [or Vikings] as they are still known in Gaelic), they increasingly came under the influence of Christianity. They are even said to have taken certain Columban traditions with them when they went to settle in Iceland.[75] The result of these changes was that Iona, what Máire Herbert called the 'umbilical symbol' of the unity of the Columban churches in Britain and Ireland, was progressively marginalised from an Irish point of view.[76] The actions of Cinaed mac Ailpín in the middle of the ninth century had a similar effect from a Scottish perspective.

Despite all these upsets, Iona remained the burial place of the Scottish kings as well as other aristocrats. Olaf Cuarán, the king of the Norse of Dublin, who had formerly been king of York, retired to Iona and died there about 980. At the end of the eleventh century Queen Margaret (later venerated as a saint), the wife of the king of Scotland, Malcolm III, is believed to have endowed the monastery, although neither she nor her husband were buried there. In 1097 the island was visited by the king of Norway, Magnus Barelegs. The *Heimskringla* saga gives a short account of the visit.

> King Magnus came with all his company to the holy island ... Men say that he asked to open the small church of Colum Cille; he did not go in but closed the door again immediately and locked it, and said that none should be so bold as to enter that church.

Throughout the twelfth century there are sporadic references to Iona indicating the continuation of an Irish-style monastery there.

7

Doire Coluim Cille:
the Monastery of Derry

The reason I love Derry
Is, its quietness, its purity;
For full of angels white it is
From one end to the other.

Attributed to Colum Cille

After the death of Fiachrach, the 'other' founder, in 620 there is no further mention of Derry in the sources until Adomnán refers to it in his Life of Colum Cille, written around 700.[77] He mentions the church and its burial ground and refers to the port as a normal place of embarkation for journeys to Britain, including Iona. In 724, Caech Sculi the scribe of Derry died. There are a few references throughout the rest of the eighth, ninth and early tenth centuries, just sufficient to let us know that the monastery continued to survive, most likely as a quiet, relatively unimportant Columban church.

In 921, Cinaed son of Domnall died in Derry. Besides a full reference to him in the annals, unusually, his personal pedigree is specifically recorded in the genealogies. He was a direct descendant of Aed mac Ainmerech, the sixth-century Cenél Conaill king who is said to have given Derry to the church. Cinaed is described in his death notice as superior both of Derry and of Drumhome in south Donegal and as 'chief counsellor of [Cenél] Conaill of the North'. If anyone is likely to have wanted to embroider the story of Aed mac Ainmerech granting Derry to Colum Cille, it would have been Cinaed. The earliest surviving version of this 'official' account of the foundation of Derry is to be found in the prefatory material to the poem *Noli Pater Indulgere* in the *Liber Hymnorum*. The date of this material is generally reckoned to be about the tenth or early eleventh century. Could it be that it belongs to the period 908 to 921 when Derry was controlled by Cinaed?

Cinaed was succeeded by Caencomhrac son of Maeluidhir who, when he died in 929, was described as abbot and bishop of the monastery of Derry and steward of the Law of Adomnán. In 952 the abbot, Adhlann son of Eichneach son of Dálach, whose father was a Cenél Conaill king, died.

Adhlann is described in the Annals of the Four Masters as the 'Guaire Aidhne of the clergy of Ireland' (Guaire Aidhne was a seventh-century king of Connacht who was considered to be an exemplar of princely generosity). Significantly, this is, effectively, the earliest use by the Four Masters of the anachronistic name Doire Coluim Cille for Derry rather than the older name, Doire Calgach.[78] Does this imply that Adhlann himself had some heightened consciousness of the Columban connections? He belonged to the Síl Lugdach among the Cenél Conaill, from the area where there was a plethora of sites associated with the early life of the saint. Just as with Cinaed son of Domnall of a generation earlier, Adhlann would have had special reasons for fostering the cult of Colum Cille in Derry.

Derry makes continuous, if sporadic, appearances in the early sources from the sixth to the end of the eleventh century. Whenever it is possible to identify the family or dynastic background of any of the individuals named in these records they can all be shown to have had Cenél Conaill links. The monastery of Derry had been founded by and on behalf of the Cenél Conaill, it retained that association even after the late eighth century when the rival Cenél nEógain secured control of all the territory around the settlement. From that time onwards Derry was a precarious Cenél Conaill 'island' in the midst of an overwhelming Cenél nEógain 'sea'. One cannot help thinking that the cultivation (and perhaps even invention) of the Columban legend was designed, at least in part, as a propaganda bulwark against the advancement of the Cenél nEógain. By the late eleventh century such a bulwark would have been collapsing. In 1100 the Norse fleet from Dublin attacked Inishowen and Derry. They were defeated by the powerful Domnall Ua Lochlainn of the Cenél nEógain, but the reference in the annals indicates that control of Derry had already changed hands. Derry was now part of Ua Lochlainn's territory; the Cenél nEógain had at last captured it. Derry had become, in effect, the capital of the Cenél nEógain.

On 10 February 1121, Domnall Ua Lochlainn, one of the most powerful men in Ireland, died. The Annals of Ulster records the following obituary for him.

> Domnall son of Ardgar son of Lochlainn, over-king of Ireland, pre-eminent among the Irish in form and lineage, in sense and valour, in happiness and prosperity, in giving valuables and food, died in Doire Coluim Cille in the thirty-eighth year of his reign, the seventy-third year of his age, on Wednesday night, the fourth of the Ides [9] of February and the eighteenth [day of the moon], the feast of Mo-Chuaróc the wise.

Domnall died in Derry where he had probably been living for much of his later years. We first hear of his association with Derry during the incident in 1100 when he defeated the Dublin expedition which had come as allies of his arch-enemy and rival for the high-kingship of Ireland, Muircertach O'Brien. Muircertach himself came to the vicinity of Derry the following year and allegedly destroyed the great hilltop fortress a few miles away, the Grianán of Aileach, which had been the symbolic headquarters of Domnall's people, the northern Uí Néill, for over five hundred years.

These events must have been connected with Domnall's move into Derry. From early in the twelfth century we see members of the king's extended dynastic line, the Cenél nEógain, being appointed to the various offices of the monastery. This was a breach with all previous tradition. Domnall had come to power amongst his own people in 1083. He was an extraordinarily dynamic chieftain who set about expanding his power base, intruding himself and his appointees wherever and whenever the opportunity arose. He was too much interested in contemporary power to be overly concerned about ancient tradition. As part of his campaign to secure the high-kingship of Ireland Domnall set about reorganising the affairs of Derry. He appointed his own people to the senior positions in the monastery, such as Congalach the son of Mac Conchaill, the *airchinneach*, 'monastic steward', who died at ninety-four years of age in 1112. In 1134, Bebhinn, a close relative of Congalach, probably his daughter, died in the senior position of *banairchinneach*, 'female monastic steward', in the monastery also. She is the first named woman in the six hundred years or so of Derry's history.

The entry in the Annals of Ulster announcing the death of Domnall Ua Lochlainn says that he died in Doire Coluim Cille, 'Derry of Colum Cille'. This is the first contemporary use in these annals of that name, although it may have appeared previously in literature. Its use here, rather than as a straightforward placename, has a literary, cultic character to it. Around the eleventh and twelfth centuries a large collection of texts purporting to have been written by or about Colum Cille came into circulation. Many of these have a Derry theme; arguing that Derry was Colum Cille's first church, the one most loved by him, the one he was saddest to leave when the time came for him to go to Iona. Words are put into the mouth of the saint in verses that are blatantly propagandistic on behalf of the Columban monastery of Derry.

> And, oh! were the tributes of Alba [Scotland] mine,
> From shore unto centre, from centre to sea,
> The site of one house, to be marked by a line,
> In the midst of fair Derry were dearer to me.

> That spot is the dearest on Erin's ground,

> For its peace and its beauty I gave it my love;
> Each leaf of the oaks around Derry is found
> To be crowded with angels from heaven above.
>
> My Derry, my Derry, my little oak grove,
> My dwelling, my home, and my own little cell;
> May God the Eternal, in heaven above,
> Send woe to the foes and defend thee well.

(trans. Douglas Hyde)

Since at least the tenth century when the *Liber Hymnorum* preface to the poem *Noli Pater Indulgere* was composed, the belief that Colum Cille had been the original founder of the monastery of Derry had been well established. The impetus for the elaboration of this claim around the beginning of the twelfth century may have been encouraged as part of Cenél Conaill propaganda in opposition to the new Cenél nEógain rulers of Derry resulting from Domnall's takeover. By demonstrating that Derry had been founded back in the sixth century by the most important of their saints, the Cenél Conaill could justifiably claim that it still belonged by right to them in the twelfth century. However, if this is, even in part, the explanation for the explosion of Columban literature in Derry around this time, it backfired. It was the new arrivals, the Cenél nEógain, rather than the ancient owners, the Cenél Conaill, who fully developed the Columban legend and made the most use of it.

Derry had developed into a busy settlement by this period with a secular as well as a monastic life. On 30 March 1135, Derry 'with its churches and houses was burned.' We know very little about its physical layout, but there are a few references in the annals to the destruction of the oak trees which gave the place its name. Some of the stories about these trees show that they were protected by ancient taboos which had originated in pre-Christian times. Colum Cille is supposed to have said:

> Though truly I'm afraid
> Of death itself and Hell,
> I'm frankly more afraid
> Of an axe-sound, west in Derry.

In 1137, Gelasius (or Gilla Mac Liag as he was known in Irish) who had been abbot of Derry for the previous sixteen years, transferred to Armagh to become the *comarba* of Patrick. Gelasius was strongly connected with the ecclesiastical reform movement which had been active in the Irish church since the beginning of the century.[79]

In the year 1150 there was a major change in Derry: the *airchinnech*,

Maelisa Ua Branain died and was replaced by Flaithbertach Ó Brolcháin, another Cenél nEógain ecclesiastic. Flaithbertach was probably the son of Mael Coluim Ó Brolcháin, the Armagh bishop, who died while on pilgrimage to the hermitage in Derry in the year 1122. Unexpectedly, on his appointment Flaithbertach was not given the title *airchinnech* like his predecessor, instead he was accorded the much more prestigious title of *comarba* of Colum Cille. For nearly one hundred and twenty years this title, and the authority over the Columban *familia* that went with it, had been reserved for the abbot of the monastery at Kells. By the middle of the twelfth century, however, Kells and the kingdom of Meath surrounding it were both in decline; the opportunity existed for Derry to take over the leadership role from the midland monastery.[80]

We don't know how the decision to transfer power from Kells to Derry came about. It seems unlikely that there was any general council or meeting of the Columban churches to arrive at a decision by consensus. A unilateral move would have been supported by the Derry-based high-king Muircertach Ua Lochlainn while the leading churchman in the country, the abbot of Armagh Gilla Mac Liag, was very well disposed to his former monastery. However the change came about, in 1158, at the synod of Brí Mac Thaidg in County Meath, Flaithbertach's position was given formal recognition and his status as the equivalent of a bishop proclaimed.

> There were present twenty five bishops with the legate of the successor of Peter [the papal legate], to ordain rules and good morals. It was on this occasion the clergy of Ireland, with the successor of Patrick, ordered a chair, the same as every bishop for the successor of Colum Cille, Flaithbertach Ó Brolcháin, and the chief abbacy over all the churches [of Colum Cille] throughout Ireland.

In 1161 a synod under the patronage of Muirchertach Ua Lochlainn proclaimed that Flaithbertach was to receive all the tribute and jurisdiction of the Columban churches in Meath and Leinster which previously had been under the control of the local lay magnates. Flaithbertach was quick to collect whatever was 'owed to Colum Cille'. Immediately on taking up office he had made a *cuairt* or official visitation throughout the territory of Cenél nEógain.

> And he obtained a horse from every chieftain, a cow from every two *biatachs* [big farmers], a cow from every three freeholders, and a cow from every four tenant farmers, and twenty cows from the king himself [plus] a gold ring of five ounces, his horse and his battledress.

He made a similar tour through Síl Cathasaigh in mid Antrim the following year when he got 'a horse from every chieftain, a sheep from every hearth, and his horse, battle-dress and a ring of gold (in which were two ounces) from their lord.' Two years later he visited the Dál Coirpre and the Uí Echach Ulad in what is now County Down. Again he received a horse from each chieftain and a sheep from each house, a *screaball* [unit of precious metal], a horse and five cows from the lord, Ua Duinnsleibhe, and an ounce of gold from his wife. In 1161 he went on a visitation to the territory of the Osraige. The tribute due to him 'was seven score oxen: but it is their value that was presented there – namely, four hundred and twenty ounces of pure silver: to wit three ounces for every ox'. Charles Doherty has drawn attention to this particular visitation, with its similarity to the claims made by Colum Cille himself on the king of Osraige in the late fictional account of the Convention of Drum Ceat found in the introduction to the *Amra Coluim Cille*.[81]

Shortly after becoming *comarba* in Derry, Flaithbertach seems to have undertaken a radical reorganisation of the physical layout of the settlement. He commenced a number of building and monumental projects. Perhaps the best known of these occurred in 1162 when with the help of 'the king of Ireland', Muircertach Ua Lochlainn, he separated the ecclesiastical precincts from the secular areas of the township which had grown up around the ancient monastery. He had to demolish over eighty houses in the process. He then constructed a stone wall around the monastery and declared a malediction on anyone who would violate it. His most important building achievement in conjunction with the king, the Tempull Mór or 'great church', was completed in 1164. This would become one of the most famous churches in the north-west of Ireland and, in the following century, would be renamed as the cathedral of the Diocese of Derry.

Flaithbertach's success in reorganising the affairs of the Columban churches in Ireland was noticed in unexpected quarters. This created something of a dilemma, as indicated in the annals in the same year that the Tempull Mór was finished:

> the leading members of the monastery of Iona, i.e. Augustin, the 'high' priest, and Dubhsidhe the Lector, and the head of the anchorites Mac Gilladuff, and the head of the *Céile Dé* Mac Forcellaigh, and the seniors of the monastery in general, came to meet the *comarba* of Colum Cille, Flaithbertach Ó Brolcháin, [to invite him] to take the abbacy of Iona, with the consent of Somerled [Lord of Argyll] and the men of Argyll and the Hebrides; but the *comarba* of Patrick [Gilla mac Liag] and the King of Ireland, [Muircertach] Ua Lochlainn, and the chiefs of Cenél nEógain prevented it.

About the same time that Derry was being reorganised physically and institutionally, the 'historians' of the settlement set about re-creating the intellectual framework against which Derry could be seen as the most important of the Columban churches in Ireland. Máire Herbert has shown that between 1150 and 1182, and almost certainly before the 'Norman Invasion' in 1169, the text known as the Irish Life of Colum Cille was written in Derry. [82] Although various older lives of the saint had been composed since Adomnán wrote his work in the late seventh century, these were all based on the latter. The Irish Life, containing slightly different material, although clearly heavily dependent on Adomnán is nevertheless 'a new literary creation'. It is written in the style of a homily to be read on the occasion of the saint's feastday, 9 June.

> Christians celebrate the festival and commemoration of Colum Cille's death on the fifth of the Ides [9] of June as to the day of the month every year, (which is) on this day today ... At that time every year, Irish scholars give a brief account of the holy Colum Cille's nobility of kin and ancestry, and furthermore of the wonders and innumerable miracles which the Lord performed for him here in this world, and of the culmination and excellent ending with which he finally crowned his victorious career, attaining his real home and his true native land, the abode of Paradise in the presence of God for ever.

One of the most important theses in the Life is that Derry was the first monastery founded by Colum Cille and the one most loved by him. If this premise could be established, there could be little or no objection to Derry assuming the leadership of the confederation of churches associated with the saint. The Life clearly sets out the story of the foundation of Derry by Colum Cille, but it also claims that he founded Kells although there is no doubt that that monastery was established in 807. The story of the Columban foundation of Derry is no more reliable. Its purpose, in this version, was to bolster the new role of leadership for the monastery there.

The Life is laid out with a clear biographical pattern. The anonymous author uses the older Latin Life by Adomnán but reshapes its material into a chronological narrative. It gathers relevant information together from the more scattered approach of Adomnán and creates a continuous story, highlighting some of Adomnán's episodes, simplifying and clarifying others, deliberately leaving out some, supplementing others and transferring the locations of some events from Scotland to Ireland. Kathleen Hughes, for example, said of the Irish Life's simpler and more direct treatment of the story of the white horse which comes to sympathise with

Colum Cille before his death that 'it is all in Adamnán, but muffled in words'. [83]

The Irish Life takes as its primary Biblical text the Lord's advice to Abraham, 'Leave your country and your land, your kindred and your own patrimony for my sake, and go into the country which I shall reveal to you' (Genesis 12:1). There follows the story of the saint's birth and early life, and then an outline of his career as a founder of monasteries in Ireland is set out in the form of a journey around the country. This is a significant new addition which goes well beyond what was written by Adomnán. Colum Cille is said to have founded many monasteries but only twelve are named: Derry, Raphoe, Durrow, Kells, Clonmore (County Louth), Lambay, Swords, Druim Monach, Moone, Assylin (County Roscommon), Drumcliff and Tory. There is also a suggestion of his involvement in the foundation of the famous monastery of Monasterboice in County Louth. This is quite unhistorical but undoubtedly reflects connections between that monastery and the *familia* of Colum Cille in the eleventh and twelfth centuries. Colum Cille is depicted as a spiritual model for his followers. Máire Herbert says of the Life that 'it caters for the demands of biography and edification, while also presenting twelfth-century aspirations in terms of the sixth-century lifetime of Colum Cille.'

A story in the Life sets out to explain how one of the greatest treasures of Derry, the *Soiscél Martain*, came to be there in the middle of the twelfth century.

> On a further occasion [Colum Cille] went from Derry to Martin's city of Tours, and brought back the Gospel which had been on Martin's breast in the grave for a hundred years, and he left it in Derry.

Saint Martin, who was a fourth-century bishop of Tours in the south of France, was greatly venerated in Ireland in the early Christian period as he was credited with the responsibility of first introducing monasticism into western Christianity. His cult was widespread, not least in the churches associated with Colum Cille. The Life of Martin by Sulpicius Severus was widely read and had been used as a model by Adomnán as well as other Columban writers. One of the high crosses on Iona was named after Martin, and in Derry there was a graveyard and a holy well dedicated to him. We might presume that some of the clearly fictional traditions associating Colum Cille and Tours might well derive from genuine historical memories associating him with Tory Island. The rendering of the name of Tours in Irish as Toirinis looks suspiciously like the name of Tory and could easily have been the cause of confusion, not to mention facilitating the deliberate exercise of poetic license.

The *Soiscél Martain* was lost in the year 1182 when it was taken by 'foreigners' at the battle of Dunbo in north County Derry. It seems to have been in use then as a battle talisman, in much the same manner as the *Cathach* in later times. This has led to a recent suggestion that the *Soiscél Martain* and the *Cathach* are one and the same manuscript. [84] The leading ecclesiastical family on Tory were the Ó Robhartaighs who may have been connected to the similarly-named Mac Robartaigh family to be found later in charge of the ancient site of Rath Cunga in south Donegal (where the *Cathach* was kept in the middle ages) and their namesakes at Ballymagroarty just outside Derry. That the honor of being 'keeper' of the shrine was not without its own dangers is indicated by the events at the battle of Belach Buidhe in 1497. The Mac Robarthaigh *maor* or steward of the *Cathach,* who had accompanied the O'Donnells against the Mac Dermotts, was slain and the shrine confiscated. It was returned two years later. Again in 1567, at the famous battle fought between the O'Donnells and the O'Neills at Fearsat Mór near Letterkenny, the Mac Robhartaigh *maor* was slain. Manus O'Donnell recounts how the *Cathach* was to be used as a talisman.

> And to open it is not lawful. And if it is borne thrice right-hand wise around the host of the Cenél Conaill when they go into battle, they come back safe in triumph. And it is on the bosom of a successor or a cleric, that is so far as may be without mortal sin, that the *Cathach* should be borne around the host.

A number of other 'relics' or objects associated with Colum Cille were used in a similar way. Mention has already been made of the *Cathbuaidh*. The *Brecbennoch* or Moneymusk Reliquary is a small church-shaped shrine which was carried by the Scots at the battle of Bannockburn in 1314.

Flaithbertach Ó Brolcháin died in 1175. He clearly had been embarked on creating a new institutional future for the Columban *familia*, with Derry as its spiritual and historically-valid headquarters. But he was too late. A few years earlier one of the most momentous events in Irish history had occurred – the arrival of the Normans in Leinster. This was to have profound implications for the *familia* or confederation of Colum Cille, as many of the most important Columban churches were located in areas which quickly came under the 'invaders' control. Together with the great, twelfth-century ecclesiastical reforms in Ireland, such as the changeover to a formal diocesan system, the impact of the Normans dealt a final blow to the possibility of the Columban church reorganising along the lines of the continental religious orders like the Augustinians and Cistercians. In 1176 Kells was destroyed. In 1179 control of the monastery on Lambay was transferred to the canons of the church of Dublin. Swords was transferred to the control of the Archbishop of Dublin, while Moone became part of the possessions of the Bishop of Glendalough. Durrow also quickly came within the Norman sphere of influence. Even Raphoe changed, when it became the seat of the Diocese of Cenél Conaill. When Gilla Mac Liac Ua Branain succeeded Flaithbertach, he was little more than abbot of Derry.

It was the ultimate paradox. For hundreds of years Derry had attempted to cultivate a reputation of pre-eminence among the Columban monasteries. In the first half of the twelfth century, Derry had been at the forefront of moves to bring the Irish church into line with the rest of Christendom, drawing it away from at least some of the more exotic traditions of 'Celtic' monasticism which had been set in train by Colum Cille himself in the sixth century. Just at the point when Derry's claims to primacy were recognised, the world it sought to lead collapsed about it, partly from the forces which it itself had set in motion.

There was one final show of strength. About 1200, Reginald son of Somerled founded a Benedictine Abbey and Augustinian Nunnery on Iona. In December 1203, a letter from Pope Innocent III sent to the Abbot Celestinus took the newly-established abbey under papal protection. A huge new building in the contemporary style was commenced on the site of the ancient monastery. There was fury in Ireland, as recorded in the annals for the following year.

> A monastery was made by Ceallach [Celestinus] in the middle of the enclosure of Iona, without any legal right and in violation of the community of Iona, and considerable damage was done to the [ancient] settlement. The clergy of the north of Ireland assembled to travel to Iona, namely: Florence O'Carolan, bishop of Tír Eoghain; Maeliosa O'Deery, bishop of Tír Conaill; and the abbot of the monastery of Peter and Paul in Armagh; Amhalgaidh Ua Ferghail, abbot of the monastery of Derry, with Ainmire O'Coffey and many of the community of Derry, as well as a great number of the clergy of the north. They went over to Iona and in accordance with the laws of the church they demolished the monastery, and the previously mentioned Amhalgaidh was ordained into the abbacy of Iona by the choice of the foreigners [the Norse of the Hebrides] and the Gaels.

It was a futile attempt to restore the ancient connection. Amhalgaidh Ua Ferghail's authority could not have lasted for long; there is no further mention of it. The Benedictine abbey was built shortly afterwards and expanded over the following centuries. It still stands as the main architectural feature on the island, obliterating, as 'the clergy of the north' feared, almost all the remains of the early Christian monastery.

The account of the expedition to stop the building of the new abbey is the last mention of Iona in the Irish annals, with the exception of one passing reference in 1249. There continued to be some contacts, of which one of the most interesting is the fifteenth century inscription recording the work of 'Donald Ó Brolcháin' on one of the capitals in the Iona Abbey church. There has been considerable discussion about Donald's identity and about parallels in the north west of Ireland with his work. One suggestion is that he may have been a monk from the Augustinian Abbey in Derry.[85]

After 1220 there are no further references in the annals to the *comarba* of Colum Cille in connection with Derry. In 1397 when it was visited by the Archbishop of Armagh, we hear of the 'monastery of the Canons Regular, called the Black Abbey of Derry'. At some stage, presumably after 1220, like many similar ancient Irish churches the community of Derry had adopted the rule of Saint Augustine. It became a house of Augustinian canons of Arrouaise, subject to the Abbey of Saints Peter and Paul in Armagh, and survived in that fashion throughout the later middle ages until the English conquest of Ulster and the dissolution of the monasteries in the late sixteenth century.

The formal position of the *comarba Coluim Cille* as leader of the saint's *familia* ended, with the end of the *familia* itself. When we next hear of this title it is being used more commonly, in connection with several of the old Columban churches. The *comarba* of Colum Cille at Drumcliff who died in 1252 was 'the richest and most prosperous man of his time in Ireland and the most esteemed, most charitable and most generous'. When Manus O'Donnell was 'enkinged' in 1537 it was 'by permission and advice of the Cenél Conaill and the *comarbadh* [successors] of Colum Cille'; probably the clergy of Kilmacrennan.

8

Colum Cille:
from the Middle Ages to the Present

> Hail Columba, most holy of saints, from the stock of the king, celebrated islander ... Father Columba, glory of our tradition, accept the prayers of your servants; save this choir that is praising you from attack by the English and assault by rivals.
>
> 14th century Scottish prayer to Saint Columba

Columban traditions of one kind and another, of course, continued in Scotland and, apparently, even in the North of England as well as in Ireland. A fourteenth-century manuscript in Edinburgh preserves the music and words for a service of lauds for the Feast of Saint Columba from the Augustinian Abbey of Inchcolm in the Firth of Forth. Parts of the music are said to date to the twelfth century and earlier.[86]

A later Scottish work, the Breviary of Aberdeen, also contains much of Columban interest. It was compiled for William Elphinstone, bishop of Aberdeen from 1483 to 1514 and was printed in Edinburgh about 1510. It includes, for example, an abridged version of the *Vita Columbae* and rare material on Finán and Colmán, the seventh-century Irish bishops of Lindisfarne. It also has an office, consisting of nine short lessons, for reading on the feastday of Adomnán, 23 September. This bears a striking similarity to parts of the tenth-century Kells text, the *Betha Adomnáin*. There is still debate about whether both are based on an original Iona composition which is now lost or, as Padraig Ó Riain argues, the Aberdeen text was based on the *Betha Adomnáin*.[87]

In 1532 the greatest of the works compiled about Colum Cille in premodern times, was completed by the Donegal aristocrat, Manus O'Donnell. Manus did not succeed to the chieftainship of the O'Donnells until his father's death in 1537. However, he had been a leading figure in Donegal since at least 1511 when he had deputised for the chieftain who was away on pilgrimage. Manus continued to play an active role from that time onwards. A recent, provocative study of his career has described him as 'Manus the Magnificent', suggesting that he was a Gaelic Irish version of the great Renaissance prince, the Florentine Lorenzo de Medici.[88] Manus certainly made an impression. There is a description of him by the English

Lord Deputy St Leger, who when he met him in 1541 was surprised to find him dressed in 'a coat of crimson velvet with aglets of gold, twenty or thirty pair, over that a great double cloak of right crimson satin, girded with black velvet [and] a bonnet with a feather, set full of aglets of gold'.

Manus like his father, Aodh Ruadh O'Donnell, was a great builder. He was responsible for the foundation of the Franciscan Third Order Regular Friary at Kilmacrennan in County Donegal. This was at, or near the site of the old church of Doire Eithne, where Colum Cille was said to have been fostered as a child a thousand years earlier. The Friary may have been intended as a sort of millenial monument to the events believed to have happened at that spot. Precisely when the abbey was founded is not clear but it is not necessary, as some have argued, that it had to await Manus's succession to the chieftainship. He had completed the construction of his castle at Port na trí namat by 1527, as the Annals of the Four Masters put it, 'despite Ó Neill and the Cenel nEógain'. The castle was built in or near the present town of Lifford, located at the point where the Rivers Finn and Mourne join to become the Foyle. The three rivers are said to be the *trí namat*, 'three enemies', of the placename. The castle may actually have been built on the County Tyrone side of the river as its main function was to act as a spearhead in the almost continuous O'Donnell wars with the O'Neills. [89] Manus may also have been involved in the construction of the castle, built by the O'Doherty's for their overlords the O'Donnells, in Derry in the early sixteenth century. He may even have contemplated a Renaissance of sorts for the settlement anciently connected with his people, Doire Choluim Cille

It was at the castle of Port na trí namat that Manus completed his *Betha Colaim Chille* or 'Life of Colum Cille'. The book is a huge compendium – an encyclopoedia – of everything that was known or believed about Colum Cille at the time it was written. For Brendan Bradshaw, its composition bears 'characteristic marks of the Renaissance spirit'. Manus had written other material. A number of love poems by him – in the contemporary *amour courtois* style – survive, including two works written after his first wife, Siobhán, Con O'Neill's daughter, had died in August 1535.

Strictly speaking, Manus did not actually write the book himself. Instead he brought together a team who collected and assembled material 'that was scattered throughout the ancient books of Ireland'. The preface states that he 'ordered the part of this Life that was in Latin to be put into Irish, and the part that was in hard Irish to be made easy, so that it might be clear and simple to understand by all.' He dictated the Life 'with his own lips' to a scribe, and he did this 'having conceived the affection and love of a brother for his high-saint and kinsman by lineage, and his dear patron that he was bound to in steadfast devotion.' Manus was very well aware that as an O'Donnell he belonged to the ancient line of the Cenél Conaill, the kin group to which Colum Cille himself had belonged a thousand years earlier. In fact, the impetus to write the Life may have been the thousandth anniversary of the saint's birth in 1521.

Interestingly no copy of the full text of Adomnán's *Vita Columbae* could be found for Manus to use, but the Derry, Irish Life was available as was a whole host of other pieces of Columban literature, including a number of books which are referred to but which are not known to survive nowadays. The main manuscript of the text, known by its Bodleian Library catalogue reference as Rawlinson B514 ff 1-60, consists of sixty vellum folios, each page 17 inches by 11 1/2 inches, followed by eighteen folios of poems on the O'Donnells. There is a portrait of the saint in the robes of a mitred abbot on the second folio and the manuscript is bound in a furry sealskin. There is a second contemporary manuscript in the Franciscan Library in Dublin.

Manus tells us in the preface that his reasons for compiling the work were 'God's honour, the raising up of Colum Cille's name, the profit of the people who read or listen to it, [his] own welfare, temporal and spiritual and the dishonour and destruction of the devil.' The Life is laid out in the normal chronological and biographical manner and is written for the most part in Irish.

It is extraordinarily detailed, with 'events' specifically localised to places and features which were known to Manus himself or could be corroborated in his time. Some of the stories he tells have what might be described as a characteristically Irish twist to them.

> Another time when Colum Cille was in Derry, a gambler and a poor man came to him. And he gave a *bonn* to the gambler and a penny to the poor man. And it seemed strange to all that he should give more to the gambler than to the poor man. God revealed to Colum Cille that everyone was amazed at this, but he said to some of them that were present that they should follow the gambler and the poor man to see what each would do with the money he had given them. And they found the gambler in a tavern drinking the value of the *bonn* and sharing it with every needy person who came to him. And this was the way that they found the poor man: dead on the road and the penny that Colum Cille had given him sewn into his clothes along with five marks. They returned to Colum Cille with the news.
>
> Then Colum Cille said: 'God let me know that the poor man had only a short time to live but even if it had been longer he wouldn't have used for himself, or anyone else, what he'd been given but hoard it as he did with the five marks. And although the

> gambler was a bad man, he didn't hoard what he got but, to the
> value of the *bonn,* he satisfied himself and the others that
> were in need. That's why I gave him more than the poor man.'

The wonder-working saint of recent folklore is already apparent. He will continue to develop into the wish-fulfilling character such as the *Colum Cille na Féile* who, in the traditional song of that name from Aranmore Island, operates on no higher a spiritual level than that of helping a young man find his true-love. However, he was not always believed to have such benign characteristics.

In the Autumn of 1566, during the course of the Elizabethan conquest of Gaelic Ulster, an English garrison set up a base in Derry, including, it is believed, in the Tempull Mór cathedral church. The following April a fire broke out and spread to the ammunition store causing an explosion which killed at least thirty people. The contemporary, Philip O'Sullivan Beare, in his *History of Catholic Ireland* claimed that the English soldiers were heard to cry out 'The Irish *god* Columba killed us all.'

Death 'through the miracles of God and Colum Cille' had frequently been reported in the annals, throughout the middle ages. In 1542 the Annals of the Four Masters records a similar incident.

> Brian Dorcha Mac Conmhidhe, son of Sólaimh, a man skilled in
> poetry and literature, a rich and affluent man who kept a house of
> general hospitality for all, died about the feastday of Colum Cille
> through a miracle of God and Colum Cille and the curse of Ó
> Robhartaigh because he had profaned and dishonoured the Great
> Cross, for he had struck it before that time.

This great jewelled cross, which was mentioned in other contemporary sources was preserved as a relic of the saint by the Ó Robhartaighs on Tory island. [90] Another jewelled cross associated with the saint is mentioned in 1584. The English Lord Deputy in Ireland, Sir John Perrot, sent William Cecil, Lord Burghley, Queen Elizabeth's Chief Secretary of State, a relic of Colum Cille which he had aquired as booty from Dunluce castle on the Antrim coast during his campaigns against Sorleyboy MacDonald. Perrot was quite sarcastic about the beliefs which the native Irish had in the efficacy of the cross.

> And for a token I have sent you holy Colum Cille's Cross, a *god* of
> great veneration with Sorleyboy and all Ulster, for so great was his
> grace that happy the man thought himself who could get a kiss of
> the said cross. I send him unto you that, when you have made
> some sacrifice unto him, according to the disposition you bear unto

idolatry, you may, if you please, bestow him [the cross] upon my
good Lady Walsingham, or my Lady Sydney, to wear as a jewell of
weight and bigness, and not of price or goodness, upon some feast
or triumph day at Court.

When the English under Sir Henry Dowcra captured Derry again in 1600,
according to the author of the *Life of Red Hugh O'Donnell*, 'they tore down
the monastery and the church, and they showed neither honour nor respect
to the great Saint [Colum Cille], for they destroyed all the ecclesiastical
edifices in the place, and made rooms and sleeping apartments of them,
and used some of them to eat in.'

But not everything could have been destroyed. When Sir Cahir O'Doherty
attacked the English settlement in Derry in 1608, according to Thomas
Ridgeway writing to Lord Salisbury, the old abbey church, the Dub Regles,
'whose timber work, either in respect of the height or in devotion to their
solemn Colum Cille, the patron of that place, and whose name they use as
their word of privity and distinction in all their wicked and treacherous
attempts, was not fired'.

The events of the late sixteenth and early seventeenth centuries in
Ulster finally broke up the systems which had preserved the cult of Colum
Cille as part of the everyday dominant culture in the north-west of the
country. The introduction of Protestantism, and the Post-Reformation
responses of the Roman Catholic church, brought an end to the traditional
forms of Christianity which, at least in some respects, dated back to the
time of the saint himself. The memory of Colum Cille was preserved in
the writings of seventeenth-century Donegal authors such as the 'Four
Masters', and John Colgan who published a printed edition of Dorbéne's
text of the *Vita Columbae* in 1647. The bulk of the saint's relics, detached
now from the contexts which had given them meaning, were removed
from their traditional locations and scattered as 'antiquities' to Dublin,
Britain and the continent.

The 'Plantations in Ulster' introduced a totally new way of living and
believing, at variance with the ancient faiths and social customs. Perhaps
surprisingly, the great new, Protestant cathedral, constructed between 1628
and 1633 in the colonial city of Londonderry, was dedicated to Saint
Columb, when we might have expected its London patrons to have named
it after Saint Paul or Saint George. Something of the ancient traditions
did survive, especially, but not exclusively, in the folk beliefs and practices
of the descendants of the pre-Plantation inhabitants in Ulster. Columban
traditions were also widespread throughout the western isles of Scotland
where many of them were collected in the late nineteenth century and
published by Alexander Carmichael in the *Carmina Gadelica*.[91]

Among the Irish folk survivals were 'the prophecies' of Colum Cille.

John O'Donovan in his early nineteenth century Ordnance Survey letters mentions a James O'Hood from around Maghera in County Derry 'a great Irish scholar, who lived about the period of the Siege of Derry, [and] was the last person to understand Columbkill's prophecies'. Versions of these alleged predictions circulated widely, and a popular edition with 'literal translation and notes' was published by Nicholas O'Kearney in 1856 with many subsequent reprints. O'Kearney, who came from near Dundalk, was himself a poet and a scribe in the Gaelic tradition but his 'prophecies' amounted to no more than rewritings, probably by himself, of some of the poems attributed to Colum Cille which had been in existence from around the twelfth century. He gave colourful, nationalist interpretations to many of the references in the poems. William Reeves, who at that time was working on his own monumental *Life of St Columba*, published in 1857, rejected O'Kearney's work, denouncing one of the so-called prophecies as 'not as old as the [1851] Ecclesiastical Titles Bill!!'

Richard Sharpe has drawn attention to the sectarian debates in the second half of the nineteenth century which followed the publication of Reeves' great work.[92] Just as with Saint Patrick, Roman Catholics and Protestants of separate traditions, in a multitude of publications produced both in Britain and Ireland, argued about the nature of Columban and 'Celtic' Christianity. Reeves himself was certainly not to blame for this, but his encyclopoediac book was useful as a quarry for the various protagonists of differing points of view.

The thirteenth hundredth anniversary of the saint's death in 1897 provided a major opportunity for such denominational display, not least in Derry where remarkable Catholic ceremonies were organised by Father William Doherty, the able administrator of the Long Tower church.[93] Ten years later Father Doherty embarked on an ambitious rebuilding programme at the church. Saint Columba's or, as it is better known, the 'Long Tower' – taking its name from the Round Tower of medieval times – was originally built in 1784, the first Catholic church in Derry since the Plantation. It was erected outside the seventeenth-century city walls in an area which was increasingly turning into a Catholic ghetto. It was built on, or close to, the site of the great twelfth-century Tempull Mór, but tradition in Derry, especially that cultivated by Father Doherty, claimed that it was the site of Colum Cille's own sixth-century church. Father Doherty claimed that the rebuilding programme, which went on between 1907 and 1909, gave him the opportunity to search for the site of the ancient monastery. The exact position of the Dub Regles was

fixed beyond yea or nay by the discovery of foundations during excavations preparatory to the erection of the present church. Father William Doherty made a careful examination of the remains and, after comparing them with the seventeenth-century manuscript maps, and [Manus] O'Donnell's description, was able to define the original outline.

The results of Father Doherty's investigations were commemorated in a series of inscribed plaques inserted into the floor of the church and the surrounding graveyard. Throughout the refurbished church, elaborate stained-glass windows, paintings, sculpture and mosaic, were used to depict the familiar stories of the saint. The building became, in effect, a translation of the ancient legend into architecture and art, a monument to Colum Cille and the traditional account of the foundation of the monastery of Derry.

Father Doherty was almost certainly wrong about his identifications. Apart from the issue of the identity of the founder, the monastic church, as distinct from the Tempull Mór, was most probably on the site occupied by the Church of Ireland, Saint Augustine's chapel-of-ease. With hindsight, it is easy to be critical of the enthusiasms of this remarkable priest but, given the mutual political and sectarian hostility of the times, it would have to be said that, at the beginning of this century, Derry Catholics would have found it difficult to admit that the site of the original Columban monastery was in modern times occupied by a Protestant church. Iona too suffered from the religious and political upheavals which swept Scotland during the seventeenth century. The Abbey gradually fell into ruins and not till the late nineteenth century did restoration, first of the Abbey Church, get under way. The Iona Community was established in 1938 by George McCloud, originally as a means of bringing young ministers and craftsmen together for the purpose of rebuilding the rest of the Abbey, in its own right and also as a symbol of the unity of 'work and worship'. Since then the Community has grown into an international fraternity whose members live in ordinary society but who have a common commitment to making Christianity relevant to the modern world.

In all the ways described and in other ways, the memory, and maybe something of the spirit and ideals of Colum Cille, have survived from the sixth century to the present day. As we mark the fourteenth-hundredth anniversary of his death we can only hope that the remaining sectarian animosities between the peoples who still honour his name will be, themselves, consigned to history. No matter what one believes, or whether one believes, we have never needed more an inspiration and a symbol like that of Colum Cille.

Notes

All study of Colum Cille has to start with the original texts purporting to describe his life.. Adomnán's *Vita* is available in several modern editions. A.O. and M.O. Anderson, *Adomnán's Life of Columba* (Edinburgh, 1961, 2nd edition Oxford, 1991), gives the Latin text as well as a translation and explanatory material. Richard Sharpe, *Adomnán of Iona: Life of St Columba* (London 1995), gives an English translation as well as copious notes on many aspects of the subject. John Marsden, *The Illustrated Columcille* (London, 1991), has a translation and a discusssion, and contains many marvellous photographs of sites and objects associated with the saint. Máire Herbert, *Iona, Kells and Derry: the history and hagiography of the monastic familia of Columba* (Oxford 1988; reprinted Dublin 1996), is the most important book on the subject, and contains an edition and translation of the twelfth-century Irish Life of Colum Cille. Thomas Owen Clancy and Gilbert Márkus, *Iona: The earliest Poetry of a Celtic Monastery* (Edinburgh, 1995), contains scholarly editions of texts (with translations) of all the early poems assiciated with the saint as well as important notes and discussion. Manus O'Donnell's *Betha Colum Cille* is available in A. O'Kelleher and G. Schoepperle, *Betha Colaim Chille: Life of Columcille* (Urbana, 1918).

1   Gearóid Mac Niocaill, *Ireland before the Vikings* (Dublin, 1972), p. 39.
2   The list is preserved in the late twelfth-century manuscript, British Museum Additional 35110, and printed in various editions of Adomnán's, *Vita Columbae*, especially Anderson, *Columba*; Sharpe,*Columba*, although the identification of Colum Cille's sisters there differs from that presented here; Marsden, *Illustrated Columcille,* where, in addition to the translation of the list, there is an excellent photograph of the original manuscript text.
3   See for instance Seán Ó hEochaidh, '*Colm Cille sa tSeanchas'*, *Irisleabhar Muige Nuadhat* (1963), pp 33-50.
4   Donnchadh Ó Corráin, 'The Historical and Cultural Background to the Book of Kells', in Felicity O'Mahony (ed.), *The Book of Kells. Proceedings of a Conference at Trinity College Dublin, 6-9 September, 1992* (Aldershot, 1994), p. 5.
5   J.H. Bernard and R. Atkinson, *The Irish Liber Hymnorum* (London, 1898), vol. II, p. 28.
6   The most recent scholarly translation of the poem is to be found in Clancy and Márkus, *Iona.* I have preferred, however, to use an older rhyming version by the 'Nun of Kenmare', Sr. Mary Frances Cusack.

7 As with most of the stories about Colum Cille, the best version is to be found in Manus O'Donnell's *Betha Colaim Chille*.

8 See note 2 above. For an account of the 're-enactment' of this voyage in 1963 see, J. Barry, *Joyful Pilgrimage* (A.P.C.K., 1963).

9 See F. McCormick, 'Excavations at Iona, 1988', *Ulster Journal of Archaeology*, vol. 56, 1993, pp 78-107, where there are comprehensive references to previous archaeological investigations on the island.

10 Clancy and Márkus, *Iona,* pp 211-22.

11 See 'Irish Life of Colum Cille' (52) in Herbert, *Iona*.

12 Full text with translation printed in W. Reeves, *Acts of Archbishop Colton in his Metropolitan Visitation of the Diocese of Derry* (Dublin, 1850), pp 109-12.

13 Marsden, *Illustrated Columcille,* p. 53.

14 See for instance, The Royal Commission on the Ancient and Historical Monuments of Scotland (RCAHMS), *Argyll Vol. 4 – Iona* (Edinburgh, 1982), p. 45.

15 Sharpe, *Columba,* p. 335.

16 Jacqueline Borsje, 'The Monster in the River Ness in *Vita Sancti Columbae*: a study of a miracle', *Peritia* 8 (1994), pp 27-34.

17 For a critical view see Sharpe, *Columba,* pp 355-6.

18 F.J. Byrne, *Irish Kings and High-Kings* (London, 1973), especially pp 110-11.

19 Máire Herbert, 'The Preface to the Amra Coluim Cille', in Donnchadh Ó Corráin, Liam Breatnach and Kim McCone (eds.), *Sages, Saints and Storytellers* (Maynooth, 1989), pp 67-75.

20 Reeves, *Columba,* p. 37.

21 See note 2 above. Sinech is said to have been the 'mother of the men of mocu-Céin', generally identified with the Cianachta Glenn Geimhin.

22 Gearóid Mac Niocaill, *The Medieval Irish Annals* (Dublin, 1975), p. 29.

23 A.P. Smyth, *Celtic Leinster* (Dublin, 1982), pp 118-22, argues strongly that Adomnán may have begun his monastic career at Durrow and may even have taught the future king of Northumbria, Aldfrith, there. However, other authors have not concurred; see for example Herbert, *Iona*, p. 48 and Sharpe, *Columba,* pp 45-6.

24 Discussed by John O'Donovan (ed.), *Annála Rioghachta Éireann: Annals of the Kingdom of Ireland by the Four Masters from the earliest period to the year 1616* (7 vols., Dublin, 1848-51), footnote under the year 1185, vol. III, pp 456-59.

25 The most recent editions of the three Latin poems mentioned here can be found in Clancy and Márkus, *Iona*. I have preferred to use an older, rhyming version of the *Altus Prosator,* of which only the 'A' and 'Z' verses have been reproduced.

26 Many of these are incorporated into Manus O'Donnell's *Betha Colaim*

Chille. J.F. Kenney, *The Sources for the Early History of Ireland* (New York, 1929, reprinted Dublin, 1979), lists 79 poems of various lengths, together with references to published editions up to his own time.

27 Mac Niocaill, *Annals*, especially pp 18-20.

28 Raghnall Ó Floinn, 'Sandhills, Silver and Shrines – Fine Metalwork of the Medieval Period from Donegal', in W. Nolan, L. Ronayne and M. Dunlevy (eds.), *Donegal History and Society* (Dublin, 1995), pp 85-148.

29 Clancy and Márkus, *Iona,* pp 96-128, provide full, scholarly text, translation and discussion. See also Chapter XV '*Amra Choluim Chille* in P.L. Henry, *Saoithiúlacht na Sean-Ghaeilge* (Dublin, 1976), where there is a translation into modern Irish with scholarly introduction and notes. The version here is based on both of these works.

30 There are detailed discussions about the subsequent abbots of Iona in Andersons, *Columba*; Sharpe, *Columba*; and especially Herbert, *Iona*.

31 For the early history of Derry see Brian Lacy, 'The development of Derry *c.*600 to 1600', in G. Mac Niocaill and P.F. Wallace (eds.) *Keimelia: Studies in Memory of Tom Delaney* (Galway, 1988), pp 378-96; Brian Lacy, *Siege City: The Story of Derry and Londonderry* (Belfast 1992, reprinted 1995), especially chapter 2; Brian Lacey, 'County Derry in the Early Historic Period', in G. O'Brien (ed.), *Derry and Londonderry: History and Society* (Dublin, 1997).

32 Maura Walsh and Dáibhí Ó Cróinín (eds.), *Cumminan's Letter De controversia paschali, together with a related Irish computistical tract De ratione conputandi* (Toronto, 1988). See also 'Review' by T.M. Charles-Edwards in *Peritia* 8 (1994), pp 216-20.

33 Scholarly text, translation and full discussion in Clancy and Márkus, *Iona,* pp 129-63.

34 Sharpe, *Columba*, p. 34; Nancy Edwards, *The Archaeology of Early Medieval Ireland* (London, 1990), p. 150.

35 Herbert, *Iona*, pp 24-5.

36 George Henderson, *From Durrow to Kells: The Insular Gospel-books – 650-800* (London, 1987), p. 13.

37 Clancy and Márkus, *Iona,* p. 14.

39 There is a vast and argumentative literature on this subject. See Henderson, *Durrow,* and, for a recent Irish perspective, Bernard Meehan, *The Book of Durrow* (Dublin, 1996).

40 Máire Herbert and Pádraig Ó Riain (eds.), *Betha Adamnáin: The Irish Life of Adamnán* (London, 1988).

41 See Sharpe, *Iona*, pp 57-59.

42 Ibid., pp 350-51.

43 Denis Meehan (ed.), *Adamnan's De Locis Sanctis* (Dublin, 1983).

44 See Herbert and Ó Riain, *Betha Adamnáin*, pp 58 and 59, on which the following is based.

45 Máirín Ní Dhonnchadha, 'The Guarantor List of *Cáin Adomnáin*, 697', *Peritia* 1 (1982), pp 178-215.

46 Marsden, *Illustrated Columcille*, p. 181.

47 Meehan, *Durrow*, note 39 above.

48 Kenney, *Sources*, especially pp 283-7 and 444-5.

49 Quoted in Dáibhí Ó Cróinín, *Early Medieval Ireland* (London, 1995), p. 216, from John V. Kelleher, *Too small for stove wood, too big for kindling* (Dublin, 1979), p. 12.

50 Clancy and Márkus, *Iona*, pp 177-92, including text and translation of *Cantemus in omni die*.

51 Herbert, *Iona*, pp 57-9.

52 Kenney, *Sources*, pp 523-26.

53 Herbert, *Iona*, chapters 4 and 5 on which much of what is written here is based.

54 There is, of course, a huge literature about the Book of Kells. See especially O'Mahony, *Kells*, as in footnote 4 above. An excellent up-to-date, summary description, and outline of some of the academic issues, can be found in Bernard Meehan, *The Book of Kells* (London, 1996). For the 'Virgin and Child' motif see Dorothy Kelly, 'The Virgin and Child in Irish Sculpture', in Cormac Bourke (ed.), *From the Isles of the North* (Belfast, 1995), pp 197-204.

55 Kenney, *Sources*, pp 550-1.

56 Henderson, *Durrow*, p. 190.

57 See Ann Hamlin, 'The Blackwater Group of Crosses', in Bourke, *Isles*, pp 187-96.

58 Herbert and Ó Riain, *Betha Adamnáin*, pp 60-1, on which the following is based.

59 See also chapter 13 in Herbert, *Iona*.

60 Kenney, *Sources*, pp 726-7.

61 Herbert, 'Preface' (note 19 above), p. 68.

62 Herbert, *Iona*, chapter 8.

63 See D.L. Swan, 'Kells and its Book', in O'Mahony, *Kells*, pp 48-59.

64 Quoted in Reeves, *Columba*, p. 323 from TCD Ms H. 2. 16.

65 Ó Floinn, 'Sandhills', pp 131-32. Brian Lacy (et al.), *Archaeological Survey of County Donegal* (Lifford, 1983), especially pp 250 and 291-4.

66 Raghnall Ó Floinn, 'Schools of Metalworking in Eleventh- and Twelfth-Century Ireland', in Michael Ryan (ed.), *Ireland and Insular Art – A.D. 500-1200* (Dublin, 1987), pp 179-87.

67 Reeves, *Columba*, pp 276-98.

68 Byrne, *Kings*, p. 162.

69 Peter Harbison, 'The Biblical Iconography of Irish Romanesque Architectural Sculpture', in Bourke, *Isles*, pp 271-80.

70 Herbert, *Iona*, p. 90.

71 See note 54 above.

72 Mary Low, *Celtic Christianity and Nature: Early Irish and Hebridean Traditions* (Edinburgh, 1996), p. 90.

73 Herbert, *Iona*, p. 282.

74 See note 26 above.

75 RCAHMS, *Iona*, p. 48

76 Herbert, *Iona*, p. 124.

77 See note 31 above.

78 To this point, the Annals only used the term once when incorrectly recording the foundation of the monastery of Derry in 535. These Annals were, of course, compiled in the seventeenth century, but it does seem significant to me, whatever the reason, that the term, which is not used again until appropriately in the twelfth century, is introduced here.

79 For the twelfth-century reforms see Kathleen Hughes, *The Church in Early Irish Society* (London, 1966), chapter 24.

80 Herbert, *Iona*, chapters 8 and 9.

81 Charles Doherty, 'Some Aspects of Hagiography as a Source for Irish Economic History', *Peritia* 1 (1982), pp 300-28.

82 Herbert, *Iona*, where there is full text, translation, notes and discussion.

83 Kathleen Hughes, *Early Christian Ireland: Introduction to the Sources* (London, 1972), p. 236

84 Ó Floinn, 'Sandhills', p. 125.

85 RCAHMS, *Iona*, p. 274, note 170.

86 Edinburgh University Library, Ms. 211. iv. See introductory notes by Isobel Woods Preece to CD album, *Scottish Medieval Plainchant: Columba, Most Holy of Saints*, sung by Cappella Nova conducted by Alan Tavener.

87 Herbert and Ó Riain, *Betha Adamnáin*, pp 36-41. See also Herbert, *Iona*, pp 170-74.

88 Brendan Bradshaw, 'Manus the Magnificent: O'Donnell as Renaissance Prince', in A. Cosgrove and D. McCartney (eds.), *Studies in Irish History* (Dublin, 1979), pp 15-36.

89 Local tradition assumes that the castle was in what is now Lifford but there is an area called 'Castletown' on the Tyrone side of the river and the use of the word 'despite' is suggestive.

90 Ó Floinn, 'Sandhills', pp 132-3.

91 The *Carmina Gadelica – Charms of the Gaels – Hymns and Incantations*, edited by Alexander Carmichael and others, was published in six volumes between 1900 and 1971. A one volume edition, representing the complete collection of translations, but without the original *Gàidhlig* texts, was edited by C.J. Moore (Edinburgh, 1992, reprinted 1994).

92 Sharpe, *Columba*, pp 95-8.

93 Excellent accounts of these events can be found in *Derry Columbkille: Souvenir of the Centenary Celebrations in Honour of St. Columba, in the Long Tower Church, Derry, 1897-99*. The 'souvenir' is, in fact, a 200 page hardback book, edited (and presumably largely written) by Father Doherty. A similar account of contemporary events in Donegal can be found in the book *'Cuimhne Coluimcille' or The Gartan Festival – being A Record of the Celebration held at Gartan on the 9th June, 1897 – The Thirteenth Centennial of St.Columba* (Dublin, 1898).